Praise for Wyatt Harris
and *Second Chance*

"Wyatt's parents did a great job raising a
Chinese child and with that, he demonstrates
the power of pos...
of family l...

—HIPO CHEN, District G... ...otary District 3520

"His adopted parents gave Wyatt complete love,
letting him better understand the second chance
in life. Then he passed down his love to help other
children with his experiences."

—WU RUOQUAN, author

"Searching for roots, meaning, and finding where
it all began originates from the curiosity to find
answers and solve the mysteries of life. Wyatt
represents a pure eagerness to find the truth and in
doing so, better understands himself."

—SUN YUE, host of Good News TV, Taiwan

Second Chance

by Wyatt Harris

© Copyright 2013 by Wyatt Harris

ISBN 978-1-938467-66-0

Published by

köehlerbooks™
an imprint of Morgan James Publishing

5 Penn Plaza, 23rd floor
c/o Morgan James Publishing
New York, NY 10001
212-574-7939
www.koehlerbooks.com

Publisher
John Köehler

Executive Editor
Joe Coccaro

*The Author is donating a significant portion of
the proceeds from this book to the Second Chance Foundation.
Second Chance was founded by the author to assist orphans in
Taiwan and China by giving them a second chance at life.*

For my mother, Midge, and father, Cal.
You have loved me from the very beginning and supported
me in all my endeavors. I owe the both of you so much for
providing me a life I can be proud of and call my own.

And for my only sister from another mother, Margie, who has
always been there for me in the good and the bad. She's been
my best friend. Thanks, sis, for the squeaky dragon.

Finally, I would like to thank Rotary International, one of the
greatest, yet least heralded, organizations in the world.

Second Chance

Abandoned in China, adopted by an American family,
he journeyed back to find his biological family.

Wyatt Harris

VIRGINIA BEACH
CAPE CHARLES

PREFACE

As I walked through the terminal exit, a mob of familiar faces and cameras greeted me. I was sweating through my cardigan sweater and started to feel overwhelmed as Chinese people swarmed me. I could not help but reflect on how I got here in the first place. What was I doing here?

A Chinese mother embraced me as if I were her own. At first I felt conflicted. I don't belong here, and these people are not my family. I don't deserve their friendship. But then another voice resonated in my heart. This is what you have been working so hard to achieve.

I felt like I was in a dream state, a trance. I was speaking, but not feeling the words being spoken. My arms were shaking, but I felt numb from my fingers to my toes. My mind drifted back to my life in the U.S., my heart wished my parents were there beside me, holding my hand. As I met these strangers one by one, the past twenty years flashed before my eyes.

When the plane landed in Portland, Oregon on September 20, 1994, my life changed. I no longer was just a number or a child awaiting adoption. I now had a family, and, soon, my own bedroom. I no longer was that child whose photo was passed from family to family, hoping they would choose me as if I were a pet in a store. It was finally my turn to be the chosen one.

Just a week before my arrival in the U.S., I first met my adoptive father, Cal, and grandfather, Richard Harris. For one week, the three of us went through the tedious process of getting to know each other. I had to cope with a white guy fawning over me, and my father had to deal with a stranger who was now his son and who didn't speak English. All we could do was smile if we were happy, frown if we were upset. Sometimes I would bite my dad or granddad when I became angry or frustrated.

I wasn't a violent kid. I just didn't know how else to communicate or display frustration. Biting has the same translation in every language. I began to feel nervous and angry that these white strangers were going to take me away. I didn't want anything to do with them, or what they had to offer. These people looked, sounded and acted different. They were kind: they brought me gifts and tolerated my biting. But I was not going to go with these people without a fight. During meals, I took every chance I had to leave their side in hope of escaping and returning to my previous caregiver.

These people, my adoptive family, brought me to a small town in Oregon and into a lifestyle geared toward, education, family, respect and competition. It took time, but I began to feel like just another American kid finding his own path in life and instilled with a love of family and agriculture. I felt comfortable and happy in Baker City, Oregon. My hometown in the beautiful Pacific Northwest was safe and welcoming. I felt accepted, loved.

There were two things, however, that made me undeniably different from many of my friends and neighbors. I am Chinese and I was born missing my left hand. Despite my physical handicap, I was instilled with confidence and felt I could do anything I put my mind to. Being the only kid with one arm at school gave me determination and an imaginary protective shell that blunted negativity.

That childhood foundation has made me more resilient to the outside world and to the absent-minded. I often say that having one arm does not limit or define me. A disability is only one aspect of a person. I learned from my parents that I control my destiny and I as a person can rein in any opportunities I see.

I was not the smartest kid in class, nor was I the kid sleeping in the back. I earned Bs and, on occasion, got an A. I was the kid in school who brought more laughs to the table than ideas.

The fact that you are reading a book written by me is a miracle. My high school English teacher never saw this coming. It's proof that determination and the right attitude can lead to wonderful accomplishments. In December of 2011, I published this book in Taiwan and China (in Chinese, of course). Soon after, in June of 2012, I graduated from the University of Oregon with a degree in International Business and Chinese Literature. It was a glorious day when I received my diploma, a long way from when I was a boy abandoned by his birth parents because he was missing part of an arm. I went from castoff to college graduate.

I hope the story of my journey inspires yours. If I have learned anything it's don't ever let anyone or anything stop you from achieving your dream. You are in command of your life; you are the pilot and navigator. So, with an open mind and uninhibited spirit, go out there and do what makes you happy.

This book is a testimony of what hope, second chances and a little bit of luck can do for a person. It is also a tribute to Rotary International, one of the finest organizations in the world. The various opportunities provided me by Rotary during my year abroad have opened my eyes and my mind.

The original four - my real family.

CHAPTER 1

Who are these white people?

On September 20th, my dad carrying me with his right arm, the three of us stepped off the plane and entered what I thought was a room full of white aliens.

I later learned the beautiful woman with dark hair who was crying and holding my hand was my new mommy. I was greeted into America by my new mom, sister, aunts, uncles, great-aunts, great-uncles and cousins. With all this excitement going around, I was not at all amused by these strangers staring and smiling at me. I wasn't at all entertained until Margie, my new sister, gave me my first present—a green dragon. As I clung tighter and tighter to the green dragon it made a loud noise. I found this toy to be quite amusing and comforting. We were both being squeezed, making noise.

My first meal in the U.S. was at a restaurant called Shari's, a home-style diner. Shari's was just a few minutes away from the airport, so it didn't take long for me to be exposed to U.S. foods. Speaking of food, my parents and relatives didn't have the slightest idea what I would want to eat. Their solution was to have each member of my family order a different dish from the menu in hopes I would pick what I wanted to eat from their plates.

So with the food ordered and a variety of choices in front of me, I had hamburgers, steak, pasta, sandwiches, soup and salads to pick from. I decided that the salad fit my fancy more than anything else. I remember picking out a big tomato from the salad and sucking out the juices and seeds inside. I don't know why, but I refused to eat the outer skin of the tomato.

If I wasn't learning how to use a fork or spoon, I was being forced to learn English. Unlike most parents who have kids in the U.S., my parents had a daunting task in front of them. They had to teach their Chinese child English! Parents seldom ever have to think of how to overcome a language barrier. However, my parents were seasoned pros at this after adopting my sister from Columbia.

When I was four years old, I of course didn't have the slightest idea what people were talking about, but that was the way I learned English. My family and family friends would just chat my ear off in English, hoping I would catch on at some point. After just a year of being in the U.S., I was speaking English a lot better and even started showing signs that I was forgetting Chinese.

The technique my parents used when I was young was brutal. I still have nightmares. They tossed me in a class full of preschoolers and sandboxes in hopes I would improve my communication skills with kids my age. Now that I look back, I feel bad for that little Chinese-speaking kid. I can see it now: kids holding up cookies and making me say ku-ki in English before I could eat one. I bet that's how I learned my snack food names so fast.

Having a class full of English-speaking kids also enabled me to make friends. I was the cool kid in the class who could speak Chinese. It wouldn't surprise me to learn I had taught my nap buddies how to say "pee-pee" or "rice" in Chinese.

After a couple of months in the U.S., I had learned some

basic vocabulary. However, I was still not at a high reading level or anywhere close to learning how to read. That's what makes this next story so cute to my parents.

In most U.S. Chinese restaurants, you're given a fortune cookie at the end of your meal. Of course inside this cookie is a proverb or a fortune. I took my cookie and cracked it open. While looking at the fortune, and not being able to read what it said, I announced to the family it said "To eat mo-r—kan-di!"

When I wasn't at Chinese restaurants making up fortunes, I would be at home or at my grandparents' house. Having my grandparents live just a block away allowed my sister and me to spend as much time as we wanted with them. During this time I was going through a really weird stage. I wouldn't talk with many people, but I would just crawl on and off people. I assume this meant I liked that person or acknowledged their presence.

My English was still very poor, so this could have been my way of showing affection. A few months after I arrived in the U.S., my Grandma Priscilla and Grandpa Richard came over to visit. Feeling very comfortable around my grandparents, I sat in Grandma's lap and started to roll around in her lap. Within minutes, my grandfather looked at me and said in a high-pitched joking tone, "Hey there, what do you think you are doing?"

I turned back to him and said in English in the exact same tone, "Hey there, what do you think you are doing?" This response put them in tears of laughter. Not only did I speak pretty clear English, but I also taught my grandfather who was boss.

Even though I was speaking English pretty well after the first year, my teacher recommended I take a special class for kids who needed extra help with language skills. I wasn't very happy about this new arrangement, but I saw little choice. So for one year I took an afternoon English class with other kids my age. Most of the kids weren't second language speakers, but they just needed extra help with pronunciation. I still needed the basics.

CHAPTER 2

Adopted, but not alone

Some of my favorite memories with my sister Margie were during the summer we lived in Baker City.

We spent countless days playing in the playhouse that my dad built for her. If we were outside, we would be in the backyard or in her tree house. There were even times during the summer when the night was just cool enough for my sister and me to sleep in the playhouse. I remember being afraid of the monsters lurking outside. Margie would sleep next to the door and by the window to be my protector.

I think Margie understood better than anybody what I was going through. She too was adopted, but she came from Columbia at the age of three. When I was little, I wanted to be with her every step of the way. Wherever she went, I trailed like a wagging tail.

Margie and I were growing up fast: one moment we were playing in the house together, and the next thing I knew, I was a nuisance to her and her best friend Megan. It was hard for me to see my best friend with someone else so often. I was a bit jealous, and at times I felt I lost a sister.

What Margie did with her friends was so cool. I would have given anything to ride my bike down the street with them. I was upset on Friday nights, when I was alone in the house with my parents watching a movie, while my sister was at her friend's house for a slumber party.

Margie has always been a very protective sister. I know when I first came to the U.S., she made a promise to our mom that she was going to do everything she could to help her little brother overcome whatever challenges he might have with his one arm. Occasionally she would block the view of a pestering child who was staring at me by standing between us. On days we had a disagreement or fight, we would always make up before we went to sleep. It was things like having her as a bigger sister that made my first few months in the U.S. so comfortable.

Margie is one of the strongest-minded people I have ever met. She, too, had to deal with the fact that her family abandoned her at a young age. When we were younger, we would joke around with each other saying that Mom or Dad loved one of us more than the other. Margie would claim that Mom and Dad loved her more because she was adopted first, but I would say Mom and Dad loved me more because they weren't happy with what they got the first time, so they tried again. It was jokes like these that created a stronger bond between us.

In a recent conversation I had with my sister, I asked her about our childhood and her favorite memory. It was the winter of 1996 and I had just gotten a 12v electric Jeep for my birthday from my grandparents. The Jeep could fit two people and went a blazing five miles an hour with a forty-five-minute battery life. The trips I would take with that Jeep were mesmerizing and unforgettable. I played in that Jeep night and day, rain or shine. I would spend most of my summer days driving it up and down our street.

It was summer of 1997 and I was entering 2nd grade. It was in the evening and was getting close to dinnertime when the phone started to ring. Mom answered as I was sitting at the table drawing when I saw a concerned look on her face. After she got off the phone, I asked her what was wrong. She said, "Your sister just got stung by a bee at the neighbor's house and wants to come home."

So I looked at my Mom and said, "Okay, don't worry. I will go get her." Knowing that my sister wasn't allergic to bees, my mother hesitatingly agreed. I excused myself from the table and ran out into the garage like Batman jumping into his Batmobile. I unplugged my Jeep from the wall and quickly put it into forward gear. Putting the pedal down as far as it could go, I made my way down the street to rescue my sister.

I arrived at the house and walked her from the neighbor's house to my Jeep. After assisting her into the passenger seat, we made our voyage back home. Unfortunately my Jeep was dramatically slowing and losing power. I had already spent most of the day driving it without a proper recharge. Never minding the fact that we could walk faster than we were driving, I managed to get my sister home so Mom could comfort her.

Margie and I were always creating forts or hideouts out of blankets, pillows, clothes, cardboard or just about anything that could be used to make a wall or roof. We would spend all week designing and thinking how we wanted the fort to look. When Friday finally rolled around, we put our plans into action. We didn't just build in our respective bedrooms; we would spend all day building forts at our grandparent's homes. If my sister and I were really good, we were allowed to keep the forts up for an extended period of time so we could make the fort even bigger!

When my sister and I weren't building forts with blankets, we would be in Grandmother Rosemary's backyard playing in the garden. Grandmother, sweet as she was, would allow my sister and me to play in the mud and make mud pies. Margie and I were really productive and could easily make ten at a time.

It was the simple things like giving a kid a stack of blankets, or if not blankets, mud and containers, and letting him explore his childhood that helped develop the person I am today.

Grandmother Rosemary had such an imagination. I know that's where I got the ability to think outside the box. She taught me not to look at one thing or object and only see one possibility, but to see endless possibilities in oneself.

Unfortunately, we lost Grandmother Rosemary to cancer when I was in seventh grade. Her passing was one of the first deaths I remember having in our family. Grandfather Dennis told my sister and me that wherever we found a penny on the ground it meant she was looking down at us. It was comforting to know that, but Margie and I still miss her very much. We miss the chaos we would cause while in her presence.

CHAPTER 3

I can do it myself

When my sister and I were very young, my parents taught us valuable lessons in life, from taking responsibility for our actions to treating others as we would like to be treated. They also taught us to take care of our stuff. We had to put toys away when we were finished playing and had to respect each other's property. In the summer of 1996, a yellow tabby cat came strolling in our yard one afternoon. The cat didn't appear to be dangerous or violent, so I crept up from behind and grabbed it. The cat didn't put up a struggle at all, in fact, it was very happy to be held and very cuddly. Seeing it had no collar, I took it inside the house and asked my mom if I could keep it. With the concerned look any mother would have when their son brings a cat into the house, she just said, "It's not your cat to keep."

She said that I needed to put up posters around the block advertising the fact that I found the cat and the owners needed to come get it. After two weeks of no phone calls, my mom and dad said I could keep the cat. We took it to the vet and had it vaccinated. I decided to name it Tiger, since it kind of looked like a small version of one. Sadly, after a month, Tiger ran away and never returned. I was devastated! I cried and I cried, saying that I took care of Tiger and it wasn't fair.

Shortly after that, my mom took me to the animal shelter to adopt a new kitten we later named Lulu. Again, luck with animals just was not on my side. Lulu got very sick along with all the other cats in the shelter, and had to be euthanized. I told my parents that I never wanted a cat again. When I was in second grade, one evening my dad asked if I wanted to accompany him to the store to buy some needed ingredients for dinner. "Yes!" I eagerly said. We pulled up to Safeway and I saw a box of puppies being given away. I jumped out of the truck and ran right over to look at the puppies. There were four puppies in the box, three white labs and one black. I picked up the first puppy that came to my hand. I held the white puppy and just gave it one big hug. After giving the puppy a look in its eyes, I turned to my dad and asked if I could get one. He simply nodded his head in approval.

I placed the white lab back in the box and grabbed the black one. At this time, the black lab was so small I could fit her in the palm of my hand. I knew the moment I grabbed her and looked into her eyes that she was the dog I wanted. When we got back home, the first thing I did was yell to my family to come outside. I remember my mom was wearing a blue sundress and my sister was in a white shirt and red shorts. I yelled to Margie, "Come look at the puppy and help me find a name for her." It didn't take long for my sister and me to each come up with a name. After hours of discussion, we finally agreed upon a name for the new puppy, "Patty Ann" from our favorite children's cartoon, Doug.

From that day, Patty was always next to us, eating or running ahead chasing cats. Whenever we went on trips, Patty rode in my dad's lap. When she got larger, she then took her own seat next to my dad. Patty allowed my sister and me to learn what it meant to care for an animal and what responsibilities came with being a dog owner. We took turns feeding her, washing her and even cleaning up the yard. Patty was with the Harris family for thirteen wonderful years before chasing her last ball in March of 2011. Having a dog and watching her grow from a small puppy into a full-size dog has been one of my proudest achievements. Patty was so much more than just a dog; she was a family member.

While Patty taught my sister and me the basic necessities of taking care of an animal, my parents wanted to instill other responsibilities into our lives than just watching after her. Both my father and mother were strong believers in doing chores and helping around the house when needed. When I was younger, the tasks included taking out the trash, helping set the dinner table and clearing it. As we got older, we took on more challenging chores, such as mowing the lawn and vacuuming the house.

The chores were simple and left us with plenty of time to play outside with our friends, most days. There were days, though, that I just did not want to clean my room or make my bed, so I didn't. I would try my best to hide the messy room by closing my door or shoving everything in the closet, but I learned you can't fool a mom forever. It worked the first couple of times, and then my mom started to catch on to my scheme. Let's just say she wasn't very happy to see I didn't put much effort into cleaning my room.

You see, back then I didn't understand why my parents made us clean our rooms. My room was my room and I thought it could be neat, dirty, smelly, moldy, or however I wanted because it was my room. My parents didn't see it the same way. They saw it as a way to respect what we have been given. "A clean room is a happy room," my mom would say. She insisted on the same show of appreciation of our toys. That meant at the end of the week, our toys should be in their proper place and clothes either hung or in the basket to be washed.

A big part of our doing chores was motivated by getting the allowance at the end of the week. When we were younger, I think we both got seven dollars a week. Of course it goes without saying that if we forgot to do a chore that day, then we didn't get that dollar for the day. As Margie and I entered middle school, we got a raise in allowance for taking on more responsibilities. By then we were starting to have a social life outside of our family, so we wanted to earn as much as we could to go places with friends and buy stuff we wanted.

During middle school my parents gave my sister and me each ten dollars a week and allowed us to do extra chores for extra spending money. For example, washing my dad's truck or mowing the lawn each paid an extra five dollars. High school was a different story for me. I didn't have time to do chores or to spend extra time trying to earn cash. I was too busy playing soccer during the fall on weekdays and weekends. During the winter, I was primarily focused on school and extracurricular activities. Then I started tennis in early February and didn't finish until late June. I had a choice to make, playing sports or earning money.

Luckily I had two wonderful parents who supported my athletic career and my extracurricular activities. After my freshman year in high school, my parents sat down with me and said, "Wyatt, we want you to participate in sports and to be active. You will have enough time to work and earn money when you get older." They were so adamant that I stay with the sports teams and enjoy my time in high school that they gave me an allowance at the beginning of every month so I would have some spending cash, gas money and even car insurance.

Yes, my parents gave me money, but they knew they taught my sister and me the value of a dollar early on in our lives. My father believed that the harder I worked to earn the money, the more rewarding it would feel once I had enough to purchase the item. Now that I look back, I see it was a valuable lesson. However, I remember there were times when I really wanted to buy something and by the time I had enough money to buy it, something newer came out.

It was a constant circle for me. I would see something I wanted and save up for it. Then when I had enough, I would see something even cooler. I really did learn the value of a dollar and the meaning of working for something I wanted. Learning the lesson "the value of a dollar" doesn't just apply to buying things we wanted, but also taught us to work hard for what we wanted. We learned that the world around us isn't just a chocolate factory giving out free candy.

Responsibility and trust were also drilled into our tiny brains from a young age. Having trust in our family was crucial and played an important role in my freedom as a child and teenager. My parents were never really big on rules or curfew. They allowed me to take responsibility for my actions and to pay the consequences if I did something wrong. For example, if I forgot to tell my parents where I was, who I was with or when I was going to be home, I knew there could be a price to pay. I never took for granted my parents' trust, and I know that's what has allowed me to be as free as I was in my childhood.

Jilli, an inspiration to me and to everyone she meets.

CHAPTER 4

Where did your hand go?

Before I reached third grade, my paternal grandparents offered my parents jobs at their beach hotel, in hopes that one day they would be able to run the hotel. So my family and I moved and started a new life in Bandon, Oregon. I really liked Bandon because it was on the coast and I would feel so free running on the beach with Patty. After a year of my parents learning the ropes and the business management side of running a hotel, my parents decided that it was not what they wanted.

Just as summer was beginning, my dad had a job interview with Two Rivers Correctional Institute in Umatilla, Oregon for a management position. He applied and got the job. Because he had to start work right away and we didn't have a place to live, my father stayed with Jan, one of his buddies from work in that area that he had known for many years while we lived with my grandparents.

It didn't take long for us to start house hunting in that area. My parents did some research and found that Hermiston was a good city to raise a family and only a fifteen-minute commute for my dad to work. I didn't really want to move from Bandon, but I had little choice. Within weeks of being in Hermiston, I registered at Highland Hills Elementary School. I was starting at a new school, with no friends, labeled as "the outcast." I was not happy at all about the new arrangement.

Who could blame me though? Right? I had just adjusted to my elementary school in Bandon, found some good friends and, with a snap of the fingers, I was in a new city and forced to smile at all the kids staring at my arm. Not to mention I was going to have to explain to them that I could do anything they could do as well. I knew it would take time to convince kids that I was just like them.

A week before classes started, my mother ran into one of her good friends of many years, Kristi Smalley. Kristi was the sister of my mom's very good friend Vicki from Baker City. So, whenever the sisters got together, they played golf. Little did I know at the time Kristi was going to be my elementary school librarian for the next two years.

Since we were new in Hermiston, it was a nice gesture for the Smalley family to invite the Harris family over for an afternoon barbecue and swim. This was the first time I met Jillian Smalley. Jilli wasn't your typical young girl. She had been diagnosed with autism at age three. Jilli has a higher-functioning form of autism, so she can play sports, draw, sculpt, and much more. She truly has a special gift that has been shared with all who have met her.

When I first met Jilli, one of the first things she noticed was my arm. She asked in her high-pitched, sweet voice, "Where did your hand go?" I just answered with, "I was born this way."

She nodded her head, and then proceeded to ask me the same question again and again. With the same response, came the same question. I just told Jilli, "This is the way God made me." It took Jilli awhile to understand that I was born special, just like her, but once she finally understood, she stopped asking me that question.

When I met Jilli, we were both age ten. Jilli was swimming in her family pool in the backyard and I was a little shy and hesitant to jump in the pool with complete strangers. However, the Eastern Oregon heat was forcing me to change into my swimsuit and go for a dip. One of the first things I learned about Jilli was her swimming ability. She was zipping from one end of the pool to the other in seconds! If she wasn't swimming from one end of the pool to the other, she was practicing her diving technique.

As the years went by, I learned that swimming was just one of her many talents. Jilli was also a bowler for the Special Olympics since the fourth grade. The Special Olympics is a worldwide organization that allows kids who have special needs to compete in Olympic-like sports. Most of these kids don't care about glory or the spotlight; all they care about is having fun and trying to make their parents proud.

Jilli's mother, Kristi, told me that bowling wasn't love at first roll with Jillian. It took time and some bribing to get Jilli to stay with the game. Bribing soon became a thing of the past. Once Jilli learned that knocking down the pins was a good thing, and that people were clapping for her, she fell in love with the sport. Just like everything Jilli sets her mind to, she succeeded and soon started to make a name for herself in the Special Olympics community.

Watching Jilli bowl has inspired not only me, but also everyone who watches her. Trust me, when I say, that she is a terrific bowler with lots of talent. Her highest scoring game is 212. With this high score, Jilli didn't become big-headed or full of herself; she just kept playing. What's most impressive is that she didn't just participate in Special Olympics bowling; she also participated in her high school bowling team. At first glance, people might have thought Jilli was going to be a burden. If so, they stopped after she threw her first ball. She could throw strike after strike while picking up spares with ease. Jilli is truly the epitome of inspiration. She doesn't bowl for fame or glory; she bowls for the love of the game. A lot of athletes can learn a thing or two from her. Jilli doesn't just know how to win: she also knows how to lose like a champ. No matter the outcome of a match, she always keeps her head high and a smile on her face.

Participating in sports side by side with Jilli, I have truly learned to never give up. The days I have a bad tennis match or feel down on myself, I just think of all the ways Jilli has overcome her challenges in bowling, cross-country skiing, basketball, baseball, bocce, and soccer. Jilli has taught me that tomorrow is another day and it will be all right. Another great thing about Jilli is that she never looks back. If she has a bad day in bowling, she is right back out there the next day playing with fresh enthusiasm. I try to apply this to my life when I have a bad day on and off the field. Because of Jilli, I always remember tomorrow is another day.

My family and I are very proud of Jilli for being a member of Team USA at the 2009 Special Olympic World Winter Games in Boise, Idaho, and the 2011 Special Olympic World Summer Games in Athens, Greece. Jilli qualified for one of the top female single bowling divisions and was a Silver Medalist.

I applaud her parents, Mark and Kristi, for letting Jilli find her roots and live her life. Just like my parents, Mark and Kristi have always provided different opportunities for Jilli to be challenged, in her school curriculum, her social activities, her after-school employment and her sports. They did not allow autism to define Jilli. Rather, they accepted it as a part of who Jilli is and encouraged their daughter to challenge herself and fully use the gifts she does have. They allowed Jilli to discover and develop her strengths instead of being bogged down by inabilities. That's a great life strategy for anyone.

Mark and Kristi didn't keep Jilli cooped up in the house before and after school. They allowed her to be a part of something bigger. They allowed her to be with the public population and they allowed her freedom, and responsibility. Mark and Kristi gave Jilli as normal a life as possible, in hopes of preparing her for the real world.

Growing up with Jilli has truly been rewarding. It's odd because people think I have been great for Jilli these past years, while the truth is that Jilli has been great for me. I know there is a reason why God gave Jilli autism, and it wasn't to make her life miserable, or her parents' job more challenging. Perhaps, it was to combine her autism and her personality together to create something much more.

In my mind, she is a special gift from God that could touch and inspire the hearts of those who have lost hope. With this gift, and watching Jilli participate in soccer during the fall, cross-country skiing during the winter, and bowling in the spring, it has inspired me to keep going in all my athletic endeavors. I look forward to seeing the bright future ahead for Ms. Jillian Smalley.

My Tennis parter and my best friend through middle school and high school.

CHAPTER 5

Milk what you have

Ever since I was old enough to join the city league sport teams, I have participated in baseball, soccer and basketball. When I was in first grade I participated in my very first sport: baseball. The main purpose was really to just learn which end of the bat to hold and try swinging a few times without throwing the bat. I remember playing baseball in Baker City during the springtime. My dad spent some extra time with me to learn how to hold the bat and to teach me the fundamentals of swinging.

Because I still have my left arm to my elbow with a little hook, I managed to grip the bat with my good right hand and hook my nub on the bottom portion of the bat. It worked out great until I got older and had to swing at a pitch instead of a still ball on a tee. Then I just resorted to manhandling the bat with one hand and swinging away with all my might while trying not to throw the bat to the pitcher.

It was about this time that my grandpa got me a book about Jim Abbott, a one handed professional pitcher. Jim would put his mitt on his nub and throw with his good hand while quickly switching the glove to the other hand right after releasing the ball. I tried that and it didn't really work as well. So I would be in the field ready to catch the ball and when it was in my glove, I would place the glove under my left arm while pulling my hand out at the same time and then throw the ball as far and accurately as I could.

In first grade, I was about three feet tall and weighed about sixty pounds. Baseball was a struggle, despite the coaching from my dad. I had trouble timing my swings.

When I was done with baseball, my parents had me try basketball. I really didn't like basketball either because it included a lot of running and throwing a ball into a small target. I struggled trying to dribble and shoot with one hand. I tried my best to stick it out and to improve on my skills, but I was not going to be Yao Ming anytime soon. If the team didn't have rules enforcing the notion that every player must play half a game, I think I would have been water boy for most of the season. My basketball career was very short-lived due less to my physical challenge to the fact that I just didn't like the sport.

Wrestling was a whole different story. I was just getting into middle school when I saw my good buddy Ben Jorgenson on the wrestling mat, practicing after school. I watched him wrestle for the duration of the practice. After getting the basic idea of wrestling, I brought up the idea of playing the sport with my parents that night. I wasn't really concerned about my dad's reaction to my recent interest in wrestling; it was my mom's I was worried about.

After getting the necessary forms signed and dated, I turned in the form to the athletic director the next morning so I could start practice that afternoon. On my first day, everybody was setting up the mats and getting the room ready for our practice.

One of the first things I did was find the coach. To my surprise, my social studies teacher, Randy, was also the head wrestling coach. I told Randy that he wasn't to worry about my one arm and that I would work as hard as I could. He showed no objections and directed me to find a warm-up partner. I found my close friend Ben stretching in the middle of the mat and asked if he would be my partner. We both were of similar build and weight, so it was a good fit.

The only difference between him and I were our skill levels. Ben had been wrestling five years. In a way it was better to have Ben as a warm-up partner because it was like having a private coach at the same time. Ben was really patient with me, as I showed no skill or coordination on the first day of practice. Halfway through the practice, I was sweating, feeling aches in my legs and back. Pushing as hard as I could to make a name for myself on the first day of practice, I kept my head held high and pushed through the pain.

From there on, it only got more difficult. However, while it may have been more challenging, I was making progress. I was starting to become loose on my feet and more focused.

During the first month, I was given a quick run-through of some basic technique and the rules of the game. Trying not to look incompetent, I just nodded my head and mirrored what I saw.

I was fortunate enough to have a father who had also wrestled in his younger years, so in the evenings after practice, my dad and I practiced moves in the living room. My dad was instrumental in helping me prepare for my first match just two months after I first took to the mat. I was nervous about that match, but my dad was reassuring, telling me over and over,

"Focus, you're ready. Do what we practiced and you will do fine."

When my time came to step on the mat, I snapped on my headgear and put on a focused, determined look. I walked to my proper spot and waited to shake the hand of my opponent. A kid my age from another middle school named Justin was going to be my first opponent. I was watching his every move when he was stepping onto the mat. Justin took one look at me and said to his coach, "He has one hand, he won't win."

I was so angry. I looked back at my father and the only thing he did was point to his head and then to his heart. The whistle blew and within seconds, I had his leg and threw him down on the mat to score two points. Still having his leg, I kept him on the ground until I saw the perfect opportunity to grab his arm. I got both his arms locked between his body and mine and held him down on his back until the referee acknowledged the pin for the win.

As the referee raised my arm in victory, I looked over to my father and smiled. Both my mother and father were on their feet cheering and screaming. That day was one of the happiest of my wrestling career, which lasted three more years and took me all across Oregon and Washington for tournaments.

I won some and lost some. What I ended up winning wasn't just a bunch of medals or trophies from tournaments. I won the respect of fellow wrestlers, coaches and teammates from all over Oregon for being the inspirational wrestler with one arm who won matches. My success was grounded in hard work, just as it was for any successful wrestler: I worked out daily, watched what I ate and got plenty of rest. I gained a lot of physical strength from those three years—and a lot of confidence.

Some wonder why I had quit wrestling after middle school instead of continuing through high school. It's a simple answer: I found another passion in life. Wrestling occupied me in the fall and part of the winter, so I still had spring and part of winter to participate in other sports.

In seventh grade, my best friend, Ian McMichael, signed up for the tennis team while I was on the track team. At first glance, tennis looked kind of wimpy compared to wrestling, so I constantly gave Ian a bad time about playing a girl sport. In the second week of track practice, we had gotten out early. So, I walked over to the tennis courts to watch Ian play that sissy sport. I was sitting outside the fence watching them rally with one another when a ball came flying over the fence in my direction.

I chased after the ball and held it at eye level for a minute. I squeezed the ball and then threw the ball in the air to drop right back in my hand. The felt on my palm was a new feeling for me. I tossed the ball back over the fence and started to think about picking up the sport just to resolve a curiosity. So that night, I went to Bi-Mart and bought a twenty dollar tennis racquet and a can of tennis balls.

I quit the track team the next day and showed up at the tennis courts with sneakers, a cheap racquet and a water bottle. I didn't just surprise Ian with my new interest in the game, but also the coach. The coach showed some concern about my ability to serve the ball. I was honest with the coaches. I told them that I had never really played before, but I was willing to learn and to put one hundred percent of my sweat and tears into learning this sport. Even though that day was my first day, it was only Ian's second week of tennis. We both were on the learning curve. Ian and I became each other's hitting partners for the following weeks.

After I showed interest in tennis for a month, my father decided to give the sport a try for himself. He found an old tennis racquet in the garage one afternoon and had the both of us practice together. Even though my dad had never played before, he watched a lot of tennis on TV and read some articles about the game. He was able to help me find different ways I could hit a one-hand backhand while helping me to develop that swing into a stronger, more reliable shot. While the task of hitting a one-hand backhand presented a challenge, the serve was our biggest obstacle.

My dad and I spent countless hours on and off the tennis court finding a way to throw the ball high enough to give me time to get the racquet cocked and ready to hit a serve. I have to admit that I was growing frustrated trying to figure out how to hit a serve with one arm. One afternoon I was playing around and holding a tennis ball when I got distracted and, without any thought, I balanced the ball on my left arm. That was it! I went home and that night I took my dad to the courts to develop this serve technique even more. I used my left arm—instead of a left hand—to toss the ball straight up. I had to work on timing and placement, but at least I had a way to serve.

Middle school tennis was a lot of fun. I learned the rules and started to develop in many different areas. My forehand and backhand were looking better and better, and my serve was starting to feel really comfortable. Ian and I paired up in seventh and eighth grades as a doubles team.

When we were freshmen in high school, we knew we wanted to play tennis for the varsity squad. So we worked hard during the off-season and made some adjustments to our game to ensure our readiness for the tennis team tryouts. What do you know, Ian and I both made the varsity tennis team our freshman year. It was quite an accomplishment for freshmen to make the team, let alone make the varsity tennis team.

Our freshman year was as different from middle school as night and day. We had an impressive record of 18-3, playing number four doubles, which meant there were three doubles teams better than us. That following summer, Ian and I knew we had a really good thing going. We knew that if we worked hard enough and changed what we needed to in our game, then we had a good chance to qualify for the state tennis tournament the following year.

That summer we worked harder and played a couple of

tournaments to scope out competition. In our sophomore year, Ian and I decided we needed a private coach to get us to the next level. So once a week, we both drove to another city to have a private tennis lesson for an hour with our semi-pro instructor Max. Max really worked with me and helped me utilize my one hand to full advantage. The extra time and effort paid off. Ian and I played number three doubles and had a 19-5 record.

Unfortunately, I took a trip to Taiwan during my junior year in high school, so Ian had to play with another partner during that year. Ian was playing all that year, while I didn't have the opportunity to play much at all. When I came back in the summer of my senior year, Ian and I got back out on the courts and started to prepare for the upcoming season. We continued to get our private lessons once a week during the winter season with Max.

At the district tournament, Ian and I won our first match with no problem. We were predicted to place third or fourth in the tournament, which would have been good enough to get us to the state championships. Ian and I wound up drawing the number one seeded team in our quarterfinal match. That was not what we had hoped for. We needed to get to the semifinals and didn't figure on meeting the number one team until the finals. Our opponents were a solid team that could go all the way. The warm-up felt good, serves were feeling comfortable and the weather was perfect for tennis. With the other team winning the flip, they served first. Ian and I were not off to a good start. We weren't on our toes, forcing us to make a lot of errors. The next thing you knew, we are down a set and had one more set to go.

We both looked at each other and shared a few encouraging words. Ian was first to serve on the second set and we thought we were regaining control for a while, but then it just didn't seem to be getting any better. At this point, Ian and I took a break and talked with each other about strategy. We glanced toward our teammates and family and gave them a look of disappointment.

We were losing one game to four. I was on serve, and started to feel the nerves radiate up and down my arm. I knew we had to win this game if we had any chance of coming back. Before I served, I shouted to Ian, "Don't worry Ian, let's do it. We might lose, but we were going to go down trying."

We dropped another game and Ian and I took a moment to discuss our predicament. We turned it into a happy moment. I told Ian how much fun it has been to play and that we just had a bad day. Then Ian said the same thing and finished by saying, "Let's go out there and just have fun." That's what we did and that's how we ended up coming back, winning the second set seven games to five. Just focusing on playing the game and enjoying ourselves removed the pressure. We relaxed, found our rhythm and were starting to play some real tennis.

The third set was our most exciting set we have ever played. We won six games to four. We were literally two points away from losing and being eliminated and somehow managed to come back to win two sets. The team, coach and our families were cheering loud from outside the fence; it was such an amazing moment for the both of us. We just could not believe we came back. When Ian and I got done hugging each other, we shook the hands of our opponents.

One of the other players was gracious. "You are such an inspiration, good game," he said. That was just the nicest thing I could hear at that moment. What an amazing day that was for Ian and me. We later went on to defeat our next opponents in two sets, advancing to the state championship tournament.

After district, it was back to training with Max. We had about a week and half to solidify our game. Our first game was great for a couple of reasons. We drew a later time bracket, so Ian and I could relax and stay rested till our match that evening. And, our match would be seven in the afternoon, when it would be considerably cooler. We ended up winning the game in two straight sets. We were pretty happy with day one results.

The second day of the three-day competition was off and

running by eight. We had a match at eleven in the morning. Before our game, Ian and I went over and hugged our families and friends who came to cheer us. Our high school even sent us messages wishing us luck in the following game.

Now it was game time. We lost the flip and they chose to serve. Due to the fact that it was an indoor facility, we didn't have a preference about sides. So we stayed on the same side. With our customary high five and fist pump before every match, we got into positions. I was going to be first to receive the serve. And I wanted to get the server's attention right from the beginning. So I stepped up a little closer to the net than I normally would. He served with a perfect toss and swung with grace through the ball. I saw the ball and the slice he put on it, planted my feet and swung back at it with the same intensity. Boom. The shot went right down the right side of the court. We were off to a great start. With the first set being neck and neck, the other team pulled away and finished the set. It was okay, though; Ian and I had come back from worse. The second set was about to start. Ian was up to serve. He was really on fire that day with accuracy and speed. Ian served ace and ace, winning us that first game in a matter of minutes. I really do think we got those teams' attention and made them see we weren't done quite yet.

The next set was another close battle. They were up a game and one point away from advancing to the semis. I was up to serve, looked at Ian and followed his sign to not poach to the other side. So, I had to make my serve wide in hopes of keeping us in the game. The ball balanced in my nub, the racquet hung from my left hand and my parents prayed that it would go well. I threw the ball high and little in front of my body and swung like I did all winter during training. The ball went in, but not as wide as I wanted. The opponent returned the shot to me, I returned the shot to his partner and with one swing and a drop shot, they had scored the game-winning point. A two and half-hour battle and three years of playing with Ian were finally over. We fought hard and did well.

I was sad we lost but not angry or feeling like a failure.

Tennis has been more than just a sport for me. It has given me the ability to see challenges and to learn how to overcome those challenges. While tennis may have had its difficult moments, my parents were there every step of the way to encourage and push me to succeed. Both of my parents had so much confidence in my tennis ability. They paid for all my new racquets, bags, equipment, private lessons, tournaments and more. I could always count on my mom and dad sitting on the bleachers rooting for me whether I was winning or losing.

They never got down on me if I had a bad day and lost. They just spoke encouraging words and offered a hug when needed. Their support and the love of the game led to a seven-year tennis career that I am very proud of. Five of those years were with Ian McMichael, who never showed any worries or concerns about having a tennis partner with one arm. Sure we had fights and debates about who was right or wrong or who messed up, but we always managed to put disagreements behind us when the time called for us to stick together.

Ian was just as supportive as my parents. I know it wasn't always easy for Ian to have a partner with one arm, but we made the changes we needed to in order to make it work. Ian would always tell me about the funny looks we get from the opponents' teammates after they watched a kid with one arm beat them. I just laughed and said, "They were in awe of how tall you are, Ian."

Whether or not I like to admit it, I find it very enjoyable when I see pedestrians walking by and stopping to watch me serve. It flatters me. I always hope that one-day someone who may have been told that they can't do something because of a physical disability or for any other reason may see me playing tennis and decide to try. I hope seeing me serve can inspire them to go out and try new things they never thought they could in hopes of discovering their true potential.

If I listened to every person who said, "No, you can't do

that because you have one arm," then I would not be who I am today. So if you know someone or something is stopping you from discovering your dreams, don't stand and wait for the wall of discouragement to move, because rude people will always say rude things. You just have to ignore what they say and milk your potential so you can achieve your dreams.

CHAPTER 6

Do I buy another arm?

Having one arm and being Chinese is everything I know. I get asked a lot if I would want to get a prosthetic arm or a hook for my left arm. I always say, "I don't need one and I don't have a reason to get one." My parents from the very beginning have always given me the opportunity to get a prosthetic should I decide I want one. They never forced me to get one and they would never made me feel guilty should I ever choose to get a prosthetic.

To be honest, there were times growing up I would look in the mirror and wish I had a second hand. I would be lying if I didn't say I ever dreamed of having two arms. There was once a time in middle school when I really liked this girl. We were good friends and I felt we got along really well. So one night at our school dance, I decided to ask her to be my girlfriend. With a sweet smile and very flattering voice she said, "I'm sorry. I don't like you like that."

I felt rejected and it hurt the whole night. I was thinking to myself, "If I had two arms, she would probably like me." Just to make the whole situation worse, my two-handed friend got a girlfriend the very next day—the same girl I'd asked the night before.

So yeah, I did have points when I was growing up that I'd wished I had been born with two hands. I soon got over the whole heartbreaking girlfriend incident, though, and moved on to another girl.

Later that year, I was just finishing my last year in middle school when I started to think more and more about getting a prosthetic. So one evening, I called my Grandpa Richard to ask for his advice. Both my grandparents and my parents stood hand-in-hand when it came to this topic. All of us knew that prosthetics were very expensive and getting one could be a difficult process. Knowing this, I was starting to feel like maybe a prosthetic was right for me. My dad, Grandpa Richard and I made a trip to a city about three hours east of my hometown to have a consultation about prosthetics. The consultation was very interesting and I learned a lot about the endless possibilities of prosthetics. However, after leaving the consultation, I looked at my father and grandfather and said, "A prosthetic arm isn't what I need or want."

When I started to get older and became more active in school and the community, I had to face the fact that I would be like this for the rest of my life. As much as my parents were there to help me to learn to cope with the challenges of having one arm, they also prepared me to learn and adapt by myself. They never spoon-fed me or treated me any differently because I had one arm. They treated me just like my sister and just like any other normal child.

They raised me to be a self-sufficient and self-motivated individual. Growing up wasn't easy, but it wasn't difficult either. It was normal. My parents, family and friends treated me like a normal person; therefore, I am a normal self-sufficient person today. I know there is no way of changing the way I look or the way I was born. The good Lord gave me two feet to walk with and two ears to listen with. He gave me a set of eyes to see the beautiful world and a nose to smell my mother's meatloaf. I am lucky enough to have been born with one good arm, so the day my wife and I have a child, I will be able to hold that precious child in my arm. To me that sounds like a normal life.

Even as the strong-minded person I have become today, I still feel a little embarrassed when I put on a suit. The feeling of having the left sleeve hung awkwardly down my side is uncomfortable. It makes me feel a little off center or in simpler terms makes me feel just weird. Having one arm doesn't just affect the final appearance of me in a suit; it also causes some other issues.

I have had to accept the fact that I can't eat a churro and hold my girlfriend's hand at the same time. I can't take her ballroom dancing without making us feel strange. I can't interlace both my hands in hers and give her a romantic kiss under the moon. Having all these romantic fantasies of being with a girlfriend makes it difficult once I think about my limitations.

One of my friends a few years back made a joke when I was dating a girl in high school, that if she was ever mad at me and didn't want to hold hands with me, all she had to do was sit on the left side of me. At that time, I thought the joke was really cruel, especially since all my friends laughed!

Since then, whenever I'm with a girl, I always find myself thinking, "Is she mad? She keeps walking on the left side of me." Generally, however, when the night or date came to an end, I always got that kiss goodnight and the chance to walk her home hand in hand.

Looking back into my life and remembering all the things I accomplished with one hand makes me proud. I'm not necessarily thinking of just sports-related activities. I am thinking of how successful and how upbeat I stayed even with my condition. Missing one hand isn't so bad when compared to people who are blind or wheelchair-bound. That seems incomparable; there are people with those conditions who have led remarkable, meaningful lives, people who have overcome those disabilities just as I have overcome mine.

I know that after all these years, that's what kept me going and allowed me to have such a positive outlook. I never saw having one arm as an issue I couldn't overcome. Those people who are blind, paralyzed, deaf, autistic or missing two or more limbs playing sports are truly amazing and inspire me to work harder and stay positive.

Some people may think that I am unlucky, but the truth is I am very lucky. I have at least one good arm to use and the ability to do anything I want to do. I may be missing part of an arm and a hand, but I have a good mind. I am fit. I have some great friends and a supportive family. And I have been able to compete in sports with others who are not handicapped. Coping with one hand has been pretty easy and a fun challenge. I had to learn, for example, how to tie a shoe with one hand and serve a tennis ball. While I may fail on the first, second and even third attempt, I will always keep trying. Giving up is too easy, and I never allowed myself to give up when something was difficult.

When times did get difficult and I was having trouble succeeding, I had no problem asking for help. Quite frankly, there are times I have to ask my parents to help me do ordinary things like cooking. Straining pasta is normally a one-person job; however, I always ask for assistance to hold the strainer while I pour. Its little things such as minute kitchen tasks that remind me I do have my limitations. I do what I can, but there is never any shame in asking for help. Trust me; I know this first-hand.

CHAPTER 7

Tending roots?

Growing up in a smaller town made it more difficult to view and participate in traditional Chinese holidays. Visits to Chinatown in Portland or Seattle were the most I was ever exposed to Chinese arts, food or people. When describing my city to people around the world, I often say it is so small that there are only five Asians in Hermiston, and four of them own the local Chen's Chinese Restaurant.

There really aren't that many Asian people in Hermiston or surrounding cities. That meant I went a large part of my life not exposed to Chinese arts, foods, or culture. I heard a little bit of the language anytime I dined in at Chen's, but for the most part, I was exposed to English and Spanish.

Every once in a while, my mom would go out of her way to bring Chinese culture to me. Whether it was making an authentic Chinese dinner, participating in Chinese traditions or just keeping me up to date on Chinese news, I could always count on my mom to help me learn more about my "birth culture."

There was one year when I was fifteen, my mom made a very traditional Chinese meal. She cooked Kung Pao chicken, sweet and sour chicken and egg flour soup. She prepared the meal in a very traditional style with Chinese dishware. It was very amusing watching my family use chopsticks as they were going after the chicken. I think my dad had a better grasp of chopsticks than my mother or sister, but he still struggled with the Kung Pao. It's odd, though: I may have forgotten how to speak Chinese but I never forgot how to use chopsticks. Thank God for that!

Following the dinner, my mom gave me a red envelope with money in it. I already knew about this tradition from my Korean friend, but I didn't know my mom knew about it. So I was really excited to receive this gift from my parents. I later tried to tell my mom that she was supposed to give me the same thing every week for good fortune, but she didn't believe me.

My parents never made my sister or me feel like we ever had to forget about our pasts. They wanted us to embrace our races and to be who we wanted to be. There was no lying to us. No matter what we did or what we ate, we were going to be Chinese and Columbian at the end of the day.

There is one birthday that I remember the most and that's when my mom handmade me a birthday card. Prior to my birthday, I taught her how to say 'I love you' in Chinese. A few weeks after telling her that, I opened my birthday card from my parents and it was a handmade card with I love you written on the front. To this day, that is my favorite birthday card I have ever received.

The most important part of my past is still with me and will always be with me, my Chinese name. The Chinese name I was given from the orphanage is my legal middle name in the U.S.: Ma WuBao. I don't know why my parents decided to keep that as my middle name, but I am really happy they did. The only problem that came from having my Chinese name and being raised to speak and write English was I had no idea how to write my name in Chinese. I didn't learn how to write my Chinese name until I went to Taiwan my junior year in high school.

It is fair to say that while both my parents encouraged my sister and me to learn about our birth cultures, my mom has played the strongest role in helping me hold onto my Chinese roots these past years. For that and everything else they've done, I love them.

The farewell party of the 2007-2008 exchange students in Taiwan.

CHAPTER 8

Exploring the world

In the summer of 2006, my mom and I were sitting on the couch watching our regular TV show, Desperate Housewives, when I saw a commercial about kids studying abroad. My eyes were glued to the television set. I was intrigued by the possibility of studying anywhere in the world for a year. After the commercial ended I looked at my mom and said, "I want to study abroad." Just smiling and half-joking my mom responded, "If you want to, you have to go through Rotary."

"What's Rot-ary?" I asked.

She went into some detail talking about the organization and the things it does. I ran to the office and Googled "Rotary." I was overloaded by information. I had not realized the scope and reach of this group. Rotary International strives to bring communities together through fellowship and good business practices, while bringing professional leaders together around the world.

When I got off the Internet and returned to the comfort of the couch, I asked my mom why she knew about Rotary and if she would actually let me study abroad. She said, "They are a great organization and your father and I would trust them."

I remembered that our family had hosted a kid from France and another from Mexico through Rotary. I don't remember Kerri-Anne from France except for stories that my sister and parents tell me. As for Mao from Mexico, I remember him pretty well. He was sixteen, very fit and got along well with anyone. I remember he would play with my sister and me some evenings, riding bikes or using our train set. I asked my mom if the program I was interested was the same one. I looked up the president of the Hermiston Rotary Club and when their next meeting was going to be held. From that point, it was a matter of filling out the proper documents and passing all the requirements.

Rotary was looking for high school sophomores who would be abroad during their junior year. We had to have a strong GPA and three recommendation letters from faculty and acquaintances. Fortunately for me, they did not require you to speak another language, but they did require that you do your best to learn the culture and the language. In Oregon and part of Washington State, there were about fifty outbound students and the same number of inbound students coming from France, Germany, Switzerland, Italy, India, Columbia, Mexico, Brazil, Taiwan, Thailand, Japan and other places. My first orientation involved meeting these other outbound and inbound students. It was the inbound students' responsibility to create a posterboard and traditional clothes to show off their country. We called this event the country fair. This way, all the outbound kids got to see what another country was like and meet someone from it.

After the country fair ended, we had a chance to mingle freely with the inbounds and learn things they might have forgotten to tell us. The following two days were pretty important, but really boring. We focused on homesickness, "culture shock" and other reactions from extended travel abroad. We basically got a crash course in how miserable we may feel while abroad and how to avoid coming home early. It was at our second orientation in January of 2007 that we got to choose our top three countries where we wanted to live. We weren't guaranteed to go to our top choice, but, you would most likely get one of the three.

I always hoped for an opportunity to learn Chinese again and would have put China first on my wish list; however, China, at that time, did not have any Rotary programs. After contemplating what other countries spoke Chinese, Chuck, a Rotarian, said that the country of Taiwan spoke Mandarin Chinese as well.

I replied, "That's great! I think going to Thailand would be great!"

Chuck looked at me and said, "No it's Taiwan."

I said, "Taiwan? Where is that?" After a brief geography lesson, I wrote Taiwan on the list, followed by Italy and France.

At the end of the orientation in La-Grande Oregon, we all submitted our wish list to the Rotarians. After all the lists were gathered, the six Rotarians convened in a conference room and deliberated which student would go where. With all fifty students gathered outside the door, we patiently waited, hoping we would get our first choice. What seemed like hours was only twenty minutes, and then the Rotarians opened the door.

They wasted no time in calling out names and announcing which country would be sponsoring us the upcoming year. When they announced my name, I was saying to myself, 'Thailand... Thailand...please Thailand.' When they announced that it was Taiwan, I had a sudden lump in my throat. It took about twenty seconds after they announced my sponsoring country to realize that I wanted Taiwan.

Because we rented out the bowling alley for our event for the whole night, no one could sleep with the all the excitement, so we just kept bowling and bowling till our arms (or half our arms) were about to fall off. The next morning I was on the two-hour bus ride back to Hermiston, where I called and told my mom that I got Taiwan.

Now that my country was picked and I had a pretty good idea of what culture shock was, I was to spend the last four months preparing for my departure. I now had to apply for a Taiwanese Visa and passport, and start learning some Chinese. My mom bought me a book with all these different facts about the Island: what to buy, what not to give as a gift, where to sit in the taxi or even how to properly introduce yourself.

I remember being very excited to go--until the last week. My mom started to hug more, my sister was being nicer and my dad was, well... just not getting aggravated as easily as he normally would be. It was obvious; my family was sad and apprehensive. We all knew during the eleven months, I would not be permitted to return to the U.S. That meant no Christmas, Thanksgiving or birthday with the family. I flew out of Portland in late July of 2007. Portland was about a three-hour drive from Hermiston and I had a really early flight, so my mom, dad, Margie, grandparents, Aunt Tia and Ian all went to the airport to send me off.

I remember meeting up with Alec and Brendan, two other outbounds who were also going to Taiwan. We said our goodbyes and marched through security without a problem. While the two other guys kept walking, I stopped and turned around and waved one last time to my family. With a big smile, I turned and proceeded through the terminal. It was hard not to cry, considering I have never been this far apart for them, let alone be in another country. It was really scary.

When I finally arrived in Taiwan at six the following day, I said goodbye to Alec and Brendan, since they were going to different cities in Taiwan, before grabbing my bag off the carousel. With my two large blue suitcases, I walked out of baggage claim and saw the man from the photo provided by Rotary. My host father, Kim, was in a suit, and his wife was in pink pants and a white shirt. Their daughter, Maggie, was eighteen and wearing a jean skirt and T-shirt. Her English was really good considering she would not be studying abroad until the following year, so she did most of the translation for us.

We stepped outside the airport and I was overwhelmed by the heat. The humidity was high and I was sweating just waiting for Kim to go get the car. My first night in Taiwan was unforgettable. I was absolutely exhausted from the long flight and lack of sleep. But, it was only six, so I had to stay up for awhile longer. I will admit, I was a bit high on adrenaline since I was now in this foreign country where everything looked so different. The airport was in Taoyuan, about an hour outside of Taipei where I would spend the following eleven months. Before I could go to bed, the family took me out to a Chinese restaurant. I couldn't read a thing on the menu and there weren't any pictures. Maggie ordered my food for me. Before the food arrived, Kim handed his wife, Maggie and me a small cup and proceeded to pour beer into our cup.

We had five rules to follow while abroad. They were the five D's. No Driving, No Dating, No Disfigurement (tattoo), No Drinking, No Drugs. My very first night, I took my very first drink of alcohol in my entire life. I didn't know how to say "no," so I took a sip and it just went from there.

My cup was empty and I felt the Asian glow in my cheeks. Food started being served. Maggie asked me if I ever had stinky tofu. I said, "No, but why is it called stinky tofu?" She said "You will know why, soon enough." About five minutes into my meal, I smell this awful stench coming from the kitchen.

I realized the smell was getting stronger as the waiter got closer to our table. Maggie laughed and said, "This is stinky tofu." I now know why it was called that, all right.

I enjoyed living with Kim and his family. Kim was a lawyer and the mom stayed at home while Maggie completed her studies. I stayed with them for nearly four months. By the end, I was able to speak a little Chinese. After Kim's family, I was with two other host families that were excellent. My second host family had more kids. I tried to set a good example by making sure my younger host brother and host sister did their homework before the parents got home.

The third family lived a bit farther away and in a more remote neighborhood. So I really had to learn how to use the public transportation systems in Taiwan. And yes, I got lost on multiple occasions. The third family didn't have kids but they kept active by playing squash every other day. All three families were Rotarians at my Host Club Zhong Shan in Taipei.

School was really different. I went from wearing jeans and a hoodie in Oregon to a school uniform of a daily basis. We were given two pairs of black dress pants, two long and short-sleeve striped button-up shirts, one long and one short-sleeve sweater and a blazer. Our P.E days, we had to wear ugly blue pants and a white shirt with a red strip running along our collar. Needless to say, I was not a fan of our P.E uniform.

There were five other exchange students at Dong Fang High. I would be lying if I said I never hung out with them. I did my best to mingle with the locals, but they were shy or, well, just reluctant to talk to the foreigners. So the exchange students and I talked a lot and would hang out.

During that year abroad, I learned a lot about myself. Living in Taiwan for a year got me thinking more about my past life in China. I couldn't believe that I was so close to China, yet felt so far away. From that year on, I started to think more and more about the possibility of tracing my roots. It was unfortunate that I was so close to China, but wasn't allowed to visit. Not worrying too much about the political conflict, I continued with my year in Taiwan learning Chinese, or, I should say, attempting to learn Chinese.

Learning the language isn't the only goal of studying abroad. Our focus was to learn and observe the culture, traditions, schools, and way of life. The biggest challenge for most exchange students was culture shock. Culture shock is simply living in a whole different society than what you grew up in or are accustomed to. I came from a very small city of seventeen thousand with no buses, no skyscrapers, no taxis and certainly not thousands of 7-Elevens. It was fair to say, it took some time for me to adjust to the different lifestyle Taiwan offered.

Just being in Taiwan, I gained a lot of self-confidence and became more independent. In the U.S., I got too comfortable having my parents always by my side reminding me what needed to be done or how to do it. The year abroad let me to become more self-sufficient and helped me grow into the mentally strong person I am today. Studying abroad has also strengthened my mind set and the way I look at life and the world. There were times when I was homesick and missing my life in the U.S. However, by staying as busy as I could and staying active in school and other Rotary activities, I soon stopped missing home as much.

Some of the lifestyle changes in Taiwan included school uniforms, public transit and sharing a bathroom with the family. The year in Taiwan allowed me to grow as a person and to find my identity. As much as we love to be with our family, we need to do that on our own. Not only did I have the confidence to move from Point A to Point B with a train, but I also matured while the year progressed. Being an ambassador of your home country, an exchange student, means being held to a certain level. You present and share home cultures with fellow Rotarians, families, and classmates. I made presentations monthly at Zhongshan Rotary Club and participated in all the Rotary activities.

The greatest parts about Rotary and the Youth Exchange

Program (YEP) were the activities held on our behalf. Chinese classes were offered to the forty-nine other inbounds on a daily basis for two hours, and trips around Taiwan were also organized. Within the first month of being in Taiwan, I had already visited major cities surrounding Taipei and had started to adjust to the new lifestyle. Every year District 3520, my district, has a round island trip for the exchange students. This trip allows exchange students to see all corners of Taiwan while trying famous delicious dishes that aren't available in Taipei.

If we weren't on a bus traveling around Taiwan then we were all together learning calligraphy, tai chi or baking in Taipei. At least once a week, all the inbounds got together to do some activity that involved public speaking, cooking, or exercising. One of the coolest activities we got to participate in was the coming-of-age ceremony. It involved having the boys wear a traditional Chinese shirt and hat while the girls wore a pink dress with a hairpin. This was just one of the many different traditional ceremonies I had the privilege to take part in.

Returning to the U.S. was bittersweet for me. I was really excited to see my parents and to sleep in my own bed again, but then I truly missed my exchange student friends. After the first month of being back in Oregon, the coming-home feeling wore off and my mom started making me do chores again. I really didn't have any problems resuming them, though. I guess I matured a little while in Taiwan and learned a thing or two about carrying my own weight.

Like many exchange students, I did face a difficult time after returning from the U.S. After the fifth month of being home, I was already back at my high school finishing my last year and missing Taiwan and all the people I met while abroad. It wasn't homesickness, but I really missed my life and the memories I made there. While I did my best to stay focused on school and to graduate with a 3.5 GPA, I kept feeling something was missing or out of place. That thing was me out of place. I was having a hard time readjusting to the U.S. lifestyle.

I was feeling distant from my friends; all my friends were still there and doing the same thing, but it was me who had changed. I matured in Taiwan and started to have a different mindset. I felt more independent—more adult. It caused a few quarrels once I got back to the U.S. and interacted with my friends. While I tried my best to catch up on all the gossip and the inside jokes, I still felt like the new kid on the block. After realizing that I couldn't fight the fact that I had changed and that there was nothing wrong with that, it got better.

Rotary provides more than just a program that assists kids in studying abroad. Rotary teaches kids the meaning of putting others above self and the power of change. Rotary's work doesn't always get recognized, but it is surely appreciated by those affected. It is very unfortunate a lot of people still have not heard of Rotary and all the humanitarian work they do in their communities. They're there; you just have to find them. Most major cities in the U.S., Europe, Asia and South America have Rotary clubs. It's just a matter of finding where they meet every week to become a part of something special. Rotary has set a strong foundation in my career path and what my future could look like. With the Rotary influence that I have been exposed to these past years, I have been inspired to enrich the lives of those in my communities and those across the seas. I know with Rotary can come change, and change can bring hope to those around the world.

CHAPTER 9

What really happened?

Five years ago, I was at our annual family reunion in Lincoln City, Oregon. This is a trip that my family and I take every year for a few days to just relax together and be with the extended family. I was fifteen at that time and had just finished my freshman year in high school. I remember this vacation in particular, because it was the first time I really thought about my first four years in China. I really wish I could tell you that a big event occurred during the summer causing me to think about my life in China, but there wasn't. I don't know what it was or why I felt the way I did at that time. All I remember was being at the vacation and playing with my cousin when a rush of emotion came over me.

I didn't say much, I just stood there looking at my cousins' faces and watching them interact with each other. At that time and place was the first time I ever said to myself, "These people aren't really my blood family; we don't share the same DNA and we don't look alike."

I just could not wrap my mind around the fact that my sister and I aren't really part of this family. But what I didn't understand was why I felt this way. All the aunts, uncles, grandparents, and all the attendees treated my sister and me just like any other family member. They showered us with love and provided tender hugs and kisses. I was embarrassed to talk about my feelings with my parents and cousins, so I kept it to myself for the duration of the trip.

I don't use the word embarrassing lightly, either. Here I was at the family reunion, with all the people that have loved me and cared for me for the past eleven years, and I was feeling like I wasn't a part of them. The rest of the vacation was really fun, just like any other year. We swam in the ocean, played games at the campsite and played poker at night. I know I speak for my sister when I say we both truly enjoyed partaking in the annual family reunions and activities.

There was one thing that happened at the end of that summer vacation that changed my perception of my current dilemma. We took a big family picture with all the cousins, aunts, uncles, parents and even dogs. There were at least thirty of us in the photo. When my Uncle Terry sent the photo to the families, I took one long look at the portrait. I took a few minutes to scan through the faces and even chuckled at a few people. This photo is really special to me and I keep this photo in my memory whenever I feel doubtful or distant from reality. I learned by looking at all these beautiful faces that we were truly one big happy family. Nothing in the world could have changed the way we all felt at that moment. Smile with teeth appeared in faces young and old, with the exception of some older folks who forgot to put in their dentures.

It was a moment of rejuvenation. I felt that burden, that pain of feeling like I didn't belong, just lift off my shoulders I realized that family is much more than shared DNA. Despite those feelings, I did find myself thinking more and more about who my biological parents were and why they deserted me the way they did. My curiosity about my birth parents wasn't just about understanding the abandonment. I also wanted to find out if I had any siblings and what happened to them. I remember there were times I imagined having a twin, a somewhat frightening thought. I couldn't imagine looking at another me or fathom the idea of the world having to deal with yet another version of Wyatt Harris.

I would joke with my mom that I shouldn't have to do chores on the grounds that I could have been a prince or from royalty in China. She would always nod her head with a dismissive smile and say, "I don't think so. Nice try." I jokingly made my case, arguing my charming good looks to my extensive array of knowledge surely proved I was of royalty. Finding my biological parents wasn't just to confirm my lineage. It would allow me to see what traits I shared with people of the same bloodline.

When I was a sophomore in high school, I was taking an English literature class. I don't remember what we did to deserve a movie that day, but we did. We watched The Jerk. The movie takes place during the late 1970's in the countryside. Actor Steve Martin plays Navin R. Johnson, a white simpleton who was adopted at a young age by African-American sharecroppers. Navin believes this his real family works with them on the farm. On his fortieth birthday realizes that there is something different about him. He asks his parents why he looks different. The parents knew sooner or later that they were going to have to explain about Navin's past.

"Navin, it's your birthday, and it's time you knew. You're not our natural-born child," the mother says.

"You mean I'm going to stay this color?" Navin responds.

After he realizes that he was adopted, he decides to go out into the real world to start his own life, where he later became a successful entrepreneur. I'm no simpleton, and my sister and I always knew we were adopted and of different races than our parents. But being different kindled my desire to step out in the world to discover who I am and what I could become.

If there is one thing that separates my sister and me from all the other kids with their biological parents, it is the resemblance. As much as I feel that my dad and I share a lot of common interests, feelings and thoughts, I know I will never look like him or have my mom's wonderful smile. No matter how much I feel like a part of the Harris/Farley family, the outside will never change, and I will never look like my parents' ancestors. What would I look like in twenty years? What health factors ran through my genes? Did my bloodline have a high rate of diabetes, cancer or high blood pressure? I tried not to think about that too much, but the questions lingered. I needed to find answers.

My real family. Midge (Mom) Cal (Dad) Colt (brother-in-law) Colby (nephew) and Margie (sister)

CHAPTER 10

Returning to the beginning

After returning from my year abroad in Taiwan, I knew that someday I would want to go back again. It was now my senior year at Hermiston High and I was really excited for the first day of class because I hadn't seen a lot of my friends in over a year. I got in my purple 2007 Saturn and took a five minute drive from my house to the high school. Just like clockwork, there were my friends leaning up against the glass by the food line all talking with each other. It was different this time though. My old clique had grown from about six to two dozen. I found Ian amongst that circle and stood next to him. I look around the circle and knew most of the people by name.

It was awkward. I felt like we no longer had much in common. Their lives and mind had whipped by and shifted, and did not intersect with mine. I didn't really know what they'd done that summer or even what they'd done during the previous year, nor did they know what I did either except study abroad. So, here I was standing in this circle with my closest friends and I didn't say a word. I didn't know what to say, or what they were even talking about. Ian did what he could to fill me in on all the minor details, but I was still lost in half the conversations.

It was like this all throughout my senior year. I would listen and smile and talk when I knew what was going on, but for the most part I just wished I was in the loop on all the stories and missed all my exchange friends from Taiwan.

Just like that, school was out and I had my honors diploma in hand with an acceptance letter to the University of Oregon. I knew if I started at U of O, I would be a sophomore because I took college courses during my senior year. At that point, it seemed like it was the most logical choice. Not to mention my cousins and relatives are die-hard Duck fans.

For most of that summer I was working at Hermiston Foods driving a combine. I would drive this massive machine up and down rows harvesting peas and lima beans in sync with five other combines doing the same thing. It was like mowing a lawn with a giant tractor. The days were long but the job had its benefits. I would see some of the most beautiful sunrises ever come over the mountain range.

At the end of summer, I had a pretty good farmer's tan and a stronger respect for peas. It was now that time when I was expected to leave the house and continue my education away from my parents. Just like every other college kid out there, I had to learn how to do laundry.

September of 2009, my parents drove me five hours to my new home for the next few years: Eugene, Oregon. Home of the

Ducks. I lived a very normal college dorm life during that year. Gained a few pounds, made some new friends, missed a few early classes, but, most importantly, had a lot of fun running through the dorm halls, carrying on.

During one of the lecture classes, a few students from the Office of International Affairs came to our class to tell us about their experience abroad. It was really cool hearing stories about these kids going abroad like I did during my junior year in high school. After class that day, I went to the Office to see if they had any programs from Taiwan. To my surprise they had NTU, National Taiwan University. I later learned that NTU is a very prestigious school that housed the elite students of Taiwan. So I figure that this was a good school with some really smart kids.

The requirements weren't too strenuous. You had to be a junior, have a 3.5 GPA, be in good standing with the school, and have supporting documents from your professors endorsing your work ethic. I filled out my application with my three essays about why I wanted to go abroad. It was just a matter of waiting for a phone call inviting me to meet with Shun, the director of the NTU program. I was ecstatic when I received a call to interview. There were only four spots in the program. The day of the interview was horrible. I didn't get any sleep and I was on edge. I wasn't quite sure what she was going to ask or if I was going to be interrogated.

After about an hour of talking with Shun, I didn't get any sort of read from her. She just said to watch for a phone call in the next few weeks to see if I got the spot. It was the longest three weeks ever. Finally, the phone rang. I was accepted into the program with two girls and one other guy, Lara, Sara and Mason.

I had about six months to get all my affairs in order, set my class schedule for NTU, get my dorm assignment, transfer the necessary funds to Taiwan and get my plane tickets and visa. It was close, but I did get everything squared away before departing for Taiwan again July of 2010. I arrived at one in the morning in the Taoyuan airport and was basically stuck there till nine waiting for the NTU shuttle bus to come pick us up.

We lived in the BOT dorms just off of campus. They were really nice dorm rooms with tile flooring and a whole bathroom. We had to buy electricity cards that went into a slot in our rooms to use any electricity. The dorms were really nice with a hotel feel. We had a receptionist who signed for all our packages, multiple keys to get into places and multiple elevator access. But the coolest part was the large lobby where a lot of people hung out. For the most part, a lot of exchange students from all over the world lived in these dorms. Each of the five buildings was exactly the same with twenty-eight floors. I met a few really nice people from France, Thailand, Germany and, of course, the U.S. in my building. We would always meet for dinner in the lobby or just bring our laptops down to study while taking multiple breaks to chitchat about the funny things we saw that day. I was now starting to settle in at NTU pretty well by early November. My classes were going pretty well, my Mandarin Chinese was improving and I was making friends with the locals. Most of my friends there were students as well, with the exception being that they were working on advanced degrees, including PhDs.

Joseph was a real close buddy of mine during that year. He came out of nowhere one morning when I was eating my breakfast in the lobby and just started talking to me. His English wasn't that good, but between English and Chinese we did all right.

Mid-November of 2010, Joseph asked me what I was going to do for Chinese New Year. I said I hadn't given it much thought. I asked what he was planning on doing during that time. He said that he was going back home to be with his family for almost three weeks. When I heard three weeks, I gave him a long staring look. I repeated, "three weeks?" He said "yah," as if I should have known that or something. I was totally oblivious to the fact that we had such a long break. Joseph said I should go do something or travel somewhere during that time. I didn't think it was that bad of an idea, but I knew I couldn't afford going back to the U.S. for such a short trip. So I started to think about what I wanted to do during that time.

I thought back to that day at my family reunion and how happy I was during that time. I was starting to contemplate surprising my family, but then I started to think about why I felt the way I did that day at vacation.

I think I felt upset because of the void in my life: I had no history or recollection of my first four years. I had no photos, no memories, nothing. So, from there I wondered to myself, what would it be like for me to return to my birth city of Ma'anshan? At that point in time it felt so right. It was nearby and I had the time. I might never have this opportunity again. Then I asked myself, Why do I really want to go back? Is it to find the truth? Is it to try and find closure? Why would I want to go back to Ma'anshan? I couldn't sleep at all that night. I kept rolling around in bed thinking about why I wanted to go back.

I went out to the lobby with my computer and headphones to call my parents in the U.S. With a hot cup of tea and my computer on the table ready to Skype, I attempted to call them. The key word being "attempted." No one picked up.

Then I got to thinking, What if I could find out more about my first four years? As I was pondering that question, that idea, I asked myself, Is this going to be a mistake? Will returning to my birth city bring more tears of pain than tears of joy? Will I be disappointed at what I see or learn about the place I once called home? Am I emotionally ready to handle whatever comes my way while in China?

Finally, my mom called me back. "Why are you up in the middle of the night on a school night?" my mom asked, obviously concerned. I laughed and said "Well. I've done some thinking. Is dad there too?" She called him over so they both could hear what I had to say.

With shaking hand and chills running up my spine, I just put it out there.

I wanted to ask my biological parents two questions: Why did they abandon me that day? Did they ever know I was adopted? I told my parents that I had a burning desire to learn the truth about my abandonment, and that I deserved to hear why I wasn't good enough.

I remember sitting in the lobby anxiously waiting for my parents to say something, or to at least acknowledge what I just told them about my asinine idea of returning to Ma'anshan.

My hand was shaking and I was feeling really scared at what reaction my parents may have toward this search for truth. I was more scared and nervous about how my mom would react. Is she going to feel upset and saddened at the idea of me finding my birth parents? Is she going to think that I am unhappy or wanting to leave the family? My mom was the first one to speak. With her soft motherly voice, she gave me supportive words of encouragement.

As every mother understands their cub, she could tell that I was upset and feeling guilty for what I had just asked. She said that her love for me would never change and understood that my love for them was steadfast. As I was wiping the tears away, my mom started to show her concerns. She pointed out that finding my biological parents was going to be very difficult and could cause a lot me a lot of pain. She asked how I would feel if I didn't find them. Would I become depressed or too upset to focus on my studies? All these were legitimate concerns, as I too understood the odds of finding my biological parents were slim.

After my mom said her piece, my dad got on the phone to share his support and the same concerns my mom just mentioned. I asked if mom was really okay and he just said, "Wyatt, this search won't affect the way your mom and I love you and it won't change the way you love us. We both know that, but it's the idea of her baby boy who she watched and nurtured these past sixteen years take a journey of this magnitude alone."

Even with all these questions and concerns lingering in my head, I decided that I would always regret not trying to find out more about my past. I told myself to be ready for the unexpected. I was truly in a state in mind in which I realized I might not find what I was looking for. I may never see the stadium where I was abandoned. The orphanage may not even be there anymore. More importantly, I may never find out the identity of my biological parents.

With my parents' full support emotionally and financially, I wasted no time the next day collecting data and starting from the beginning. Data collecting was very difficult and time-consuming. Because I was in Taiwan when I started planning, I didn't have any of the adoption forms or other official forms. That meant there were a lot of late night phone calls discussing what documents would be important or worth taking a closer look at. All I knew for certain was the next six weeks would be very busy.

When Margie and I came to America, neither one of us really had any belongings. We came with what was on our back or what could fit in a small bag. Margie came in a traditional Columbian dress and I in red pants and a white shirt. Once we got stateside and grew out of those clothes, my mom started what I like to call our "life box." In these boxes are photos of the adoption, adoption papers, clothing, ticket stubs, etc.

Because the documents were in Chinese, I never really focused too much on them. However, I now had a better grasp on Chinese, so I could translate what I could and then have Joseph help me with the parts I didn't understand.

When the documents were being sent to me from the U.S., I asked Grandpa Richard to send me any materials he saved from his trip to China when he and my dad came to adopt me. He sent me photos, a story of his trip and a couple of sticky notes with names and addresses. The first thing I did was read the story my grandfather typed up about the trip. It had been a long time since I've read the letter, so it helped being able to read it again, but not to the extent I needed. It was the photos he sent me that helped most. With some of the photos he took, he attached their Chinese names. The sticky notes in the package were phone numbers and the address of a translator named Adam based out of Ontario, Canada. He had assisted my father and grandfather in the completion of the adoption process. I was really excited to have a phone number and an e-mail address to work with. So the first thing I did was send Adam a two-page e-mail reminding him of my father and grandfather and explaining my intentions. After I sent the e-mail, I dialed the Canadian number anticipating hearing an older man's voice on the other end. Instead of hearing the man I had hoped would be Adam, an automated female voice said the number was no longer in use. My first dead end.

About a week after I received my grandparent's data package, I received my parents' documents. Inside were a few photos and some documents in Chinese. I didn't waste any time translating the documents and writing down important dates, locations and names. The first document I translated was the orphanage's report on the abandonment and the police station's brief report. I learned from this document that I was found on March 18, 1991, in Ma'anshan Stadium. The Yangjiashan Police station handled the missing child report and escorted me to the orphanage shortly after.

The document concluded with, "No family has yet come forward claiming the baby." There were two versions of this form, one in Chinese and the other in English. After reading the Chinese version, I took a peek at the English version. I don't know why, but they called me a girl all throughout the English version. I found that kind of entertaining and offensive at the same time. I know I had really beautiful cheeks and a wonderful baby smile, but how could they mistake me for a girl?

The second document in Chinese was the birth certificate. It seemed like a very normal birth certificate, with name, age and sex. I really couldn't get too much from the birth certificate besides the obvious. If I did get anything from that certificate, it was my birth date, December 20, 1990. Seeing that the certificate stated my birthday, I was curious as to how they knew my age or what methods they used to determine it.

I now had all the official documents I was going to have access to before I went to China. I didn't think we had much information to go from, but I was determined to find more clues somewhere, somehow. After the second week of preparing, I was able to identify the location in which I was found, the date on which I was abandoned and a name of a welfare institute in Ma'anshan.

Being totally honest in retrospect, I really didn't think we had any good leads that would help identify my biological family. With that said, I didn't plan a long-term schedule while in China. I knew I was going to have two weeks to spend in Ma'anshan, if needed. However, with the information I had in hand, I could have easily finished in two days. For all I knew, I could have found out that the orphanage I was from moved to a different province or city, so I didn't make any long-term arrangements prior to arriving.

Throughout the six weeks I had to prepare for the journey, I had a lot of time to think about my life and what this trip was going to mean. It's kind of funny how I prepared for this trip to find my biological parents, but I never once thought about what the first things I was going to say to them were going to be. During the last six weeks before my departure, more and more of my friends were becoming aware of my trip back to China. The number one question asked from family and friends was, "Aren't you mad at them for leaving you?"

I always responded with, "That's a good point, they did leave me, but for a reason I still don't understand." There was no reason to be angry or bitter toward the family for their actions that day. I can't be angry once I see what I have been provided with. It would just seem childish to hold a grudge.

However, before leaving on the grand adventure, I took some time to think about my true feelings toward the family. If there were any feelings or emotions toward the family I wanted to express, it was that I forgive them. I can't even begin to fathom the guilt the family must feel when they think back to that day. All I knew was, should I find the biological family, I wanted to leave providing the parents with a sense of relief in their hearts.

I could only wish and pray that the family can find a way to forgive themselves for what they did. I want to let the family know with all my heart that I forgive them and I appreciate what they did that day. Because I know if they didn't leave me that day, I wouldn't have the same life I do today.

As the date was getting closer and closer to my trip back, I took a couple of looks at a map to find where Ma'anshan was located. When I finally found the city on the map, I tried to find the nearest airport or major cities surrounding Ma'anshan. Actually, I was so unprepared for the beginning of the trip that it is embarrassing to talk about. I had no plans for the first day or even the slightest idea how I was going to get to Ma'anshan from the Nanjing Airport.

After the third week of researching, I asked my parents if they wanted to go to China with me. My mom couldn't, but my dad was really interested. My Aunt Tara Stevenson wanted to join us. I would meet them in Beijing on January 24th and we were going to travel around the city for a week. I would spend the second week alone on my quest in Ma'anshan. With the schedule set, VISA ready, it was the night before I flew out that I started to pack my bag. I had just bought a large green hiker's bag that could hold up to fifty pounds. I wasn't quite sure what I was going to need, so I packed a few pants, shirts, socks, boxer briefs, toothbrush, camera and my documents.

Beijing was a lot of fun for the three of us. We did what every tourist does: we walked a portion of the Great Wall, saw the Forbidden City, visited various museums and, of course, ate a bunch of different foods.

On the night before my aunt and father were going to return to the U.S., we shared a bottle of wine in the hotel lobby discussing my upcoming trip. I didn't have much to tell them about my itinerary or where I was even going to stay the first night in Ma'anshan.

My aunt and father both shared the same feelings toward my solo trip. They both were supportive and yet sincerely worried how I was going to feel or react should my trip end in disappointment.

Before the trip even started, I told all my family and friends in the U.S. that I wanted to do this out of mere curiosity. I wasn't trying to find my biological family in pursuit of new parents or new best friends. I tried my best to explain that I was not going to become angry or upset should the trip end in failure. I simply said to them that walking the streets in the city I was born in was a big achievement.

When all was said and done, it was really nice having my family and friends looking after me. The morning I was going to Nanjing Airport, my aunt and father were returning to the U.S. I gave my aunt a hug and said, "I love you guys very much." Then I turned to my dad and gave him a big hug. When all the hugs were exchanged, my dad looked at me before walking away and said, "Go find what you're looking for, and don't forget we love you very much."

He Li Juan and I at a local cafe the day after I met her in the airport.

CHAPTER 11

Back in my hometown of Ma'anshan, China

Before the plane even touched down in Nanjing, I was already starting to feel a bit woozy and nervous about the trip. I really had no idea how to get from Nanjing to Ma'anshan. I didn't know if it was going to be expensive or how long it would take to get there. Honestly, I was not well prepared, and I had to deal with the consequences of that the second I exited the terminal.

I walked around the airport for thirty minutes or so to look at a few maps and to get a gist of the surroundings. While on my journey to explore the airport, I came across a lady cleaning up the floor. Clearing my voice, I interrupted and asked her in

Chinese, "How do I get to Ma'anshan?" She gave me a glare that could cut through glass. I repeated my question and hoped she would finally understand it. With a nod of approval, a really wide grin, and her broom in her right hand, she pointed toward Exit 5.

I got in line to purchase my bus ticket to Ma'anshan. I was patiently waiting when I heard a young woman behind me cause a commotion. I looked back and saw her scrambling to find something in her purse. I must admit, I had to take a second look, she was very beautiful and I was starting to feel this trip was no longer a waste of time or my parents' money. With a very light demeanor, I asked if everything was okay. Looking up to see I was staring at her, in a shy voice she said she was trying to find her money.

My attention was quickly drawn back up front. The ticketmaster asked for my destination and then for my money. Before giving him the latter, I asked how long it was going to take to get to Ma'anshan from here. In an annoyed voice, he yelled "One hour," and then motioned for the next customer to step forward. I took my ticket, turned around, smiled and told the woman, "Good luck."

Trying not to stick out like a sore thumb, I found a seat in the corner of the waiting room. I sat there for about five minutes before I noticed the same woman was sitting in the opposite corner. I grabbed my bag and inconspicuously introduced myself to her.

After basic introduction, He Li Juan noticed my accent and asked where I learned my Chinese. After I told her Taiwan, she immediately assumed I was Taiwanese. I corrected her by saying, "No, I'm Chinese-born." After giving her my background and telling her a little about my trip to Ma'anshan, she talked a little about herself as well. It turns out He Li Juan, age twenty-seven, was working in Shanghai and taking a few weeks off for the Chinese festivities to be with her family.

We somehow got lost in conversation when an announcement

came over the intercom calling for all passengers going to Ma'anshan to go outside and find Bus 15. About a dozen passengers headed for the exit to find the bus. I boarded the bus as He Li Juan was placing her luggage in the storage compartment underneath. I wanted to be seated first to leave the decision of who to sit with up to her.

As every other passenger started to file in, I was crossing my fingers no one else was going to sit next to me. He Li boarded and sat next to me—my lucky day. Grinning as she sat down, she picked up our chat where we had left off.

On the bus, we talked about China, Ma'anshan, weather and the surroundings. She was like a tour guide, pointing out landmarks. She asked me about my quest and how I was going to do it. My answers were vague, because I still didn't know. While we were on that topic, I asked her if she had heard of Ma'anshan Welfare Institute. She thought for a second and mentioned one place that could have been it. She wasn't quite sure that place still existed. She asked for me to hold on and called her mom. Her mom said that she knew there was a welfare institute, but just didn't know where. As I was saying thank you, He Li Juan interrupted me and said, "We are here now." I turned around and looked out the window. We were on a highway but only going what felt like forty miles an hour. Brown taxis were starting to surround the bus, motorcycles were weaving in and out of traffic and bikes with fruit on the back zipped by. KFC, Pizza Hut and McDonald's signs were starting to sprout everywhere.

As He Li Juan and I exited the bus, I asked if she could recommend a hotel or a safe place I could stay at for the night. She pointed toward Crown Plaza and then gave me her phone number. She waved goodbye and disappeared in the crowd of people in the streets.

Here I was, back in my hometown, but it didn't feel that way. Most of us consider our hometown to be the place where we were born, but it's not. It's where you can go and be with family and friends and never feel like an outcast or stranger.

Hometown is that idea or a feeling that you miss while you are away for an extended time. Your hometown is what you are familiar and comfortable with. As I was walking down the street in Ma'anshan, I felt alone and out of place. I was an outcast that nobody knew. I found a bench outside of McDonald's and took a seat to arrange all my belongings. I pulled out my camera and headphones to do some recording. After I zipped my bag back up, I strapped on my backpack and started walking. As I was walking, I was recording my thoughts and feelings.

Most of those thoughts and feelings were positive. It was mainly my first impressions, current feelings on being back and how I felt about the trip so far. Once I actually said, "I made it back to Ma'anshan," I smiled and was thankful to have had this opportunity to be there.

When I began feeling like my legs couldn't take anymore walking, I checked into the first hotel I saw that looked decent and safe. After I got all settled in and in a change of clothes, I found the computer center and proceeded to look up some more information about Ma'anshan. After just minutes of being on the computer, I started to see the strict regulations China government had on Internet sites.

I was trying very hard to locate an address or phone to the orphanage in Ma'anshan. With no luck at all finding any websites pertaining to this facility, I went to the counter and made small chitchat with two young girls who were on shift.

I spent about five minutes describing what an orphanage was and why I was looking for it. It wasn't reassuring when one of them had a puzzled look on her face and responded, "Ma'anshan doesn't have an orphanage," or "I'm not familiar with this." It was about that time when the other girl got off the phone and started to write a number and address for me on piece of paper. She instructed me to call them or go there tomorrow. Feeling relieved that I was getting somewhere, I was starting to finally feel like I was in the right place. With a number in hand and a physical address to visit, I was happy to call it a day.

Still not very familiar with the city, I tried my best to stay in the vicinity of my hotel to ensure I didn't get lost. I was feeling very hungry and very generous as well. Just the warm hearts of He Li Juan and the two girls from the computer center blew me away. If there was one thing I learned while growing up, it's to appreciate the help that has been given.

I waited for half an hour in the Pizza Hut line and ordered one large pepperoni pizza with extra cheese. With the warm sizzling pizza in hand, I walked back to the computer center and asked if the girls would take a break and enjoy a few slices of pizza with me. It did take some convincing, but after seeing the extra layer of cheddar cheese, they could not resist. The girls had just ordered chicken bites and fish on a stick, so we shared our food and had a really nice conversation.

We talked about school, work, law and our backgrounds while we feasted. Next, I found the nearest convenient store to buy a beer. For one dollar I bought two bottles of Tsing Tso beer. With beer in hand, full belly, I called it a night by watching local TV before dozing off around eleven. So far, so good.

The front office of the Welfare Institute in Ma'anshan.

CHAPTER 12

If I weren't adopted, what would life be?

I knew the likelihood of finding my biological parents was low, but I had high hopes of finding the orphanage. Whether they remembered me or not was a whole different story. Before departing for Ma'anshan, I really didn't give much thought how it was going to feel to return. All I was thinking about was where the orphanage was located and if it was still going to be there.

The next morning after breakfast, I returned to the room, fell back asleep and woke back up after a couple of hours and decided to move on. I checked out, got in a taxi and handed the driver the piece of paper the girls had given me the night before. A simple nod of the head, and we were off to see the orphanage.

Getting to the orphanage was not as easy as anticipated. I did, however, see some parts of the city I don't need to see again. After countless turnarounds and what I thought to be arrivals, the taxi driver announced our real arrival. As I was sitting on the right side of the back seat, he pulled up to what appeared to be an abandoned schoolyard. What once used to be beautiful with colorful painted walls was now just faded away with broken toys rusting. I asked him if he was sure this was the orphanage. He nodded as if he wasn't sure.

As he pulled away from the yard, he got out of the car and made conversation with a local gentleman who was sweeping his part of the street. With the fare toll getting higher, I was wondering when the taxi driver was going to come back into the car to either take me back to the hotel or to another destination. A few minutes later, the taxi driver returned with a high amount of energy and said, "I know where now."

Our journey took us up a mountain. One moment I saw nice paved roads with businesses, and the next I saw abandoned buildings with trash-filled lots. I was beginning to feel we were going nowhere. Every kilometer we drove struck my heart harder and harder as the reality was starting to set in. But what seemed like hours was only thirty minutes before we arrived at a gated compound. After exiting the taxi, I looked at the meter and paid my fare. Satisfied with where I was, I directed the driver to leave. I stared at this large gate for about a minute wondering if this was actually the orphanage.

After I gave the gatekeeper a smile and wave, he opened the gate, and I made my way into the compound, with my camera in one hand and my papers under my other arm. At first glance, it was nothing like what I expected to see. It was a very well-kept place with flowers, trees, clean grounds and some old people. It was obvious this place had a groundskeeper maintaining it on a weekly basis.

As I was walking through the compound, I didn't see kids

running around or hear kids screaming; instead, I saw old people. Some were exercising and some were smoking while the others were cleaning their clothes outside. I was starting to feel upset and scared because what I feared the most was looking like a reality.

This place was no longer an orphanage. It was simply a retirement facility. I was going to turn around and leave when I heard a baby cry from a distance. Not quite sure where the noise was originating from, I followed until it got louder and louder.

As the cry was becoming more distinct, I stumbled across a sign with "baby district." written on it. At that moment, I felt a sense of achievement that's indescribable. The sound was coming from the second floor. I was so excited and nervous to take those two flights of stairs, but I knew it was going to be memorable.

As I walked up the two flights of stairs, I took a left and started heading toward the fourth door to the right. It was an entrance to a room full of babies! I couldn't believe it. Out of twenty-six infants there, only one baby had been crying, and it was that one who guided me to this place. After walking in, I could hear crying coming from the third crib on the right. I glanced at her for a moment and put my finger in her little hand and said, "Hey, you." As I was shaking her little hand, she looked up at me and gave me the cutest smile ever. Playing with her little belly, I could see she had a cleft lip and was very skinny.

I took a look around and realized in the room next door were three ladies feeding other babies. Shortly after arriving, I made my way to the other room and with a shy, quiet voice, trying not to startle them, I introduced myself with my Chinese name. After I repeated my name a second time, one of the caretakers turned her confused look into a happy smile.

She smiled and kept repeating my name really loud while calling in some other workers. I couldn't believe it; these caretakers remembered who I was. Still in shock, I was standing on one side of a room with three ladies just smiling and staring at me. I asked, "You remember who I am?" She replied, "Of course, Ma WuBao."

I found myself wiping a tear away and hoping this moment would never end.

As I started to walk toward them, I wiped my eyes with the sleeve of my shirt and just kept staring at them. I didn't know what to say. What was I supposed to say? I couldn't believe it, these caretakers remembered me. They were so curious about my whereabouts and what I was doing with my life. One of the ladies came up to me as if we had known each other for years and started to play with my nub. She was getting a feel for how it had grown these past years.

After answering a few of their questions, it was my turn to ask a few. "Was I loud as a kid?"

The woman I was asking just giggled and said, "Yes!" I also asked her what I was like as a baby. She responded, "Very funny and a cute baby." She continued to say that I would always hang out with the girls while ignoring the boys in the yard. It seems that the young Wyatt isn't so different today.

With the questions out of the way, I walked around to each crib to personally look at the babies. Their ages ranged from two months to six years old. It was really sad to see these beautiful babies alone in the cribs. These kids had such innocence in their eyes and I could feel their loneliness every minute I was holding their hands.

Almost all of the kids had some physical defect or mental problem, and some were malnourished. While walking around and observing their conditions, I began to think that's why I was there too. I was just like these kids; I had a defect my family didn't want to deal with.

All the kids were covered and wrapped in their warm blankets and ready for their lunch. There was one boy, age six, who caught my attention at first glance. He was the oldest of the children.

He was not in a crib nor was he being socially active. He was sitting at a small table by the entrance, just minding his own business. I walked over and said, "Hello." He was very shy and hesitant to respond, at first, but after I gave him a piece of gum, he decided I was an okay guy. This kid was truly one of a kind; after I helped him unwrap the stick of gum, he saw my camera around my neck. He poked at the lens a couple of times to see what it was. I noticed his attraction to my camera, so I put the camera strap around his neck and showed him how to take a picture. After I explained what to look through and how to frame the picture, he quickly got the idea and started to take some interesting photos.

Returning to the orphanage was a roller coaster for my emotions and my heart as I started to see what my life looked like for me just sixteen years earlier. Every moment I was at the orphanage, I just kept thinking to myself, what if. What if I hadn't been adopted, what would my life be like?

Exploring my birth city in a very traditional way.

CHAPTER 13

The past coming back into my life

After an hour at the orphanage, one of the caregivers asked me to stay around for a few more minutes to meet someone special. She didn't say who, but she said I would want to see this person. Within minutes I had the pleasure of meeting a man with a face as old as mine, and a body half my height. At this time, I wasn't quite sure who he was or what the commotion was all about.

After a few minutes of discussion and introductions, I learned that back in my days at the orphanage the both of us were quite close. Mazhenjie would come and play with me. Mazhenjie was now age twenty-five and owned a small printing company. I later learned that Mazhenjie lived in a government-sponsored place called Sun Village for most of his teen years before returning to the very orphanage we were both at. At Sun Village, he was with other kids in his situation and with parental figures. Unfortunately, Mazhenjie was never adopted and lived in dorm-size rooms at the welfare institute until his job could support housing on its own.

As a child, the only memory I had of China or of the orphanage is a photo taken with a caretaker and me in it. I didn't know who she was, but I assumed she was someone special. In a majority of photos my grandfather took, she is in the photo hugging me, embracing me or laughing with me. My thoughts of her from the very beginning were always good, but I couldn't remember any instances in which we interacted. My father told me from a very young age that I was just fascinated with her and I didn't want to leave her sight. On the day she was handing me over to my dad and grandfather, I was so angry and scared that I bit the poor lady on the cheek.

I always wondered if I was ever going to get a chance to meet her in person. As the kids were starting their afternoon naps, I thought it was the best time for me to make my exit. After quietly saying goodbye to the caregivers, I told them that I would see them again, soon. As I was leaving, one of the caregivers told me to arrive the next morning at 8:30. With a simple nod, I closed the door behind me and went down the stairs and out the gate.

With a basic idea of where I was, I walked down the mountainside trying to find the main road in hopes of catching a taxi. I stood along the highway for about thirty minutes waiting for a taxi, but none were to be seen. I put the camera away, tied my shoes a little tighter and backtracked. I couldn't believe it: not a single taxi was available. If I did see a taxi, it had a customer already.

I walked for two hours along the highway. I saw maybe fifteen cars go by. Just as my feet were starting to get sore and the sun was beginning to set, I had reached the outskirts of Ma'anshan.

I was at a crossroads that could have led me anywhere. I had two options: go straight for God knows how long or take a left and hope for the best.

I ended up deciding I wanted to get off the highway, so I ran across the road to start walking on the other side. I went inside the first building I saw and asked for the nearest hotel. Thankfully, there was one just ten minutes away. Finally arriving there, I pushed the button on the glass door to open it and proceeded to check in. At that point, I didn't care how much it was going to cost; I just wanted a room with a bathroom and a bed. I had a few options, but I took the single king-size bed with a computer for twenty dollars. It's a good deal. I figured having the computer would let me send emails to my family and friends back home.

After I checked in and dropped off my bag, it was almost seven and I hadn't eaten lunch yet. I was too tired to get in a taxi and find a restaurant, so I just walked along the road of the hotel, hoping to find a hole-in-the-wall restaurant that had decent food. Unfortunately, I wasn't able to find one and ended up walking about a mile before saying "Screw it" and settling for the pistachios stand. With a half-pound of pistachios for my dinner, I turned back for the hotel. On my way back, I saw down an alley a guy smoking outside a small store. I saw some dry noodles hanging from the outside, so I assumed that they sold various products.

I greeted the owner and proceeded to look around the store to find something more substantial than pistachios. It was such a small store I had to settle for dry ramen and an expired Coke. Back at my hotel, I ate my ramen half raw and chewed on pistachios between bites of noodles. After my dinner, I turned on the computer and started to tell my friends and family all that has happened thus far. Around 11:00 PM, I was still hungry, but too tired to care. I turned out the lights and passed out 'til the next morning.

It was the third day in Ma'anshan when I found myself waiting in an office for the caregiver in the photos to arrive. I couldn't believe it; I was going to meet the mysterious woman in all my photos. As I sat next to the door with the photos in my lap and a cup of hot tea in my hand, I was contemplating if I should give her a hug, formally shake her hand or simply nod.

As I was trying to take long deep breaths, I saw the doorknob turn and heard the door slowly creak open. As the warm smile I remember from the photos appeared just inches from me, I stood there in awe. I was thinking I wanted to give her a big hug and say thank you for all she did, but I just stood there like a vegetable and nodded my head. Once my adrenaline level started to go back to normal, we had a very nice conversation. After talking about the past and my four years at the orphanage, we decided to talk about the present. I discussed my objectives for this trip and what I was searching for. When all was said and done, I got a few more ideas on how I could find what I seeking. She suggested that I start to utilize radio and TV. It's funny, because I had never really given much thought to using media, but I didn't think that was a bad idea.

Before departing, we took a photo together while holding one of the photos from sixteen years earlier. So here I was, all one hundred and fifteen pounds, sitting on the lap of the caregiver, holding what used to be our last memory of each other. It was just at this point that I knew I had succeeded way beyond imagining. As she walked me out, she generously invited me to have Chinese New Year's dinner with her family before I left China. With a gracious smile, I told her I would take her up on that offer.

When I left the orphanage that day and arrived back at the hotel, I had gotten a phone call from Mazhenjie asking me to join him for lunch. He arrived at my hotel and patiently waited for me to finish getting ready. We rode in a van, along with four others. Mazhenjie was in the passenger's seat and there were two other people in the back.

Once we arrived at the restaurant, Mazhenjie did his best to explain where we were and why we were here. Not completely understanding his reasoning, I was able to understand that it was an annual lunch held in honor of all public servants in the Welfare Institute. The restaurant had been rented out for the day and there were about 100 or so attendees. There were about twenty circular tables and a stage for performances at the front of the room. Following Mazhenjie, we sat in the front by the stage on the very right next to the window.

As Mazhenjie directed me to take a seat, there were blank stares from those wondering who I was. I introduced myself and told them my connection to their city. As I completed my introductions, the other attendees acknowledged my presence with a welcome back and questions. I did my best to make small talk with the people sitting next to me, but I was still having a difficult time understanding how these young kids about my age were already working for the Welfare Institute.

It turned out these kids didn't work for the Institute; they were in the Welfare Institute program. These kids were just like me, except they haven't been adopted. During the meal, I met a lot of people, some still orphans, some adopted and some administrators from the orphanage. As the meal progressed, Mazhenjie took me around the room to introduce me and to pay respect to other attendees. The other guests were very welcoming when finding out that I had returned, and wished me the best of luck in finding my biological parents.

Completing our rounds, we returned to our table. The meal had now been going on for about two hours. Every one of those kids was funny, outgoing, talkative and respectful. They seem to have all learned these qualities by relying on each other for the past twenty years.

I learned that these kids didn't need parents or siblings; all they needed was each other. It was truly amazing seeing these kids interact. There would be moments during the meal where

I didn't feel sad for them and their misfortune. Instead, I was feeling proud and happy to be in their presence. They are truly remarkable adults considering the hand that they were dealt.

Lunch ended and Mazhenjie, two others and I got onto some electric bikes and made our way to the house of someone special. The three other kids addressed her as Mother as we entered her beautiful home. I quickly introduced myself to her and before I could repeat my name, she remembered me. "Mother" was in her mid-fifties and had her granddaughter, age five, visiting her that day. Mother brought out a freshly brewed pot of oolong tea and biscuits for us to enjoy while we caught up. During our hour of conversation, the granddaughter was drawing pictures of animals and having me guess what type. Even though I didn't know what she was drawing, I guessed a few animals I knew how to say in Chinese.

Once we left Mother's house, the kids wanted to take me to a special place that would give me a better idea of the meaning behind our names. After a short scooter ride, we arrived at a park with three stone horses that appeared to be running wild. After I took a few pictures of the stone sculpture, Mazhenjie went into detail about why the orphanage gave me the name Ma WuBao. He explained that all the kids in the orphanage have the same family name, "Ma." And that it's integrated into their full names. For me, my name translates into "Ma" meaning horse, "Wu" comes from the word warrior, and "Bao" means baby. With all of us having the same family name, it felt like we were family. Not to mention, the city we were in was "Ma'anshan."

It's a miracle how these people I had just met brought new memories to my life that I will never forget. Words can't even begin to describe how much of a privilege it was to interact with them. To hear their stories and to learn about the challenges they faced over the years and how they overcame them is nothing but breathtaking and inspiring.

As I had the honor of getting to know each individual more

personally, I seemed to find myself in more awe each time we talked. If there was one thing that impressed me the most, it was the way they treated me. They didn't treat me like a stranger or the new kid in town. They treated me with respect and looked at me as if I was one of them.

Before we left the park, we got into a four-person paddleboat and floated in the pond next to the statue. Mazhenjie was having a hard time reaching the pedal and staying on the seat, so he was walking back and forth telling us how we should paddle harder. It was a very memorable experience to say the least. Back at the hotel, He Li Juan, the girl I met on the bus, called to check in with me and to see how the search was going. I gave her a quick summary of everything and she asked if I wanted to meet her at a coffee shop around six. As she was telling me the address, I had to run downstairs for the clerk to copy down what she was saying. I wanted the clerk to write it, so I could just get in a taxi and give him or her the piece of paper.

When I got off the phone, I realized I didn't have much time to get ready. I quickly jumped in the shower, brushed my teeth, got dressed and ran down to fetch a taxi. I handed the gentleman the address and we were off.

I saw her standing outside the coffee shop waiting for me. As we entered the coffee shop, the waiter asked which we wanted, a table or a booth. We said it didn't matter, and then the waiter asked if we would like the booth with the closed curtains. Trying not to laugh or look immature, He Li Juan pointed to the table near the window. We took our seats and ordered our beverages. It was a nice, relaxing conversation without too many awkward silences.

After the glasses were empty and the bill was paid, I waved down a taxi for her. It appeared I was in the heart of the city, I thought I would walk around for a little, seeing what was around. I was about to make a decision that would change the rest of my life.

The final days with Lisa. We were in a cafe talking about everything we had accomplished.

CHAPTER 14

I swear, I didn't do it

After walking about five minutes, I came across a radio station with a six-foot steel gate surrounding the building. I noticed the gate was partially open.

I wasn't sure if I should enter or what I could accomplish by going in. If I went in, who I was going to talk to? Then again, I couldn't find a reason why I shouldn't go in and try. I was hoping that maybe, just maybe I would meet someone who could help promote my story or get me going in the right direction. Against my better judgment I passed by the unattended guard gate and walked in.

I walked into the lobby of the twenty-two-story building and stared at the elevator button. Not knowing where I was going, I randomly chose the sixth floor. Once the elevator came to a stop I peeked my head out of the elevator and said in a quite faint voice, "Hello." Hearing no response and seeing just darkness, I quickly closed the door and prepared to pick another floor.

Without giving it much thought, I pushed the 2nd floor button. As the elevator came to a stop and the door opened, I peeked my head out of the elevator and said in a quite faint voice again, "Hello." Hearing nothing but the sound of a fan, I started to feel chills up my spine. I closed the door and decided to call it a night.

As I was exiting out the door I came in from, something looked different. The door in the gate I walked through was closed completely. I tried unsuccessfully to pry it open. After 15 seconds of my prying and praying, a man opened the window from the guard gate and instructed me to come over. Not wanting to cause a commotion or any problems, I asked him nicely to open the door so I could leave.

Even with a "Please" he wasn't going to open the door. Once he saw my insistence and heard my Chinese accent, he demanded to see my ID. I told him I didn't have my passport with me, it was back at my hotel room. His angry looks and loud voice were just the beginning of what seemed like a long night ahead for me. Still yelling at me, he stepped out of his booth and walked toward me. He was an inch or two taller and about fifty pounds heavier than me. I could no longer understand what he was saying.

I backed away as he got closer and said, "I'm sorry, I'm American, I was born here, I don't have any identification on me, I'm just trying to find my biological parents." He could see that I was backing away from him when he pulled out a phone from his pocket and called the police.

Just seconds after hearing the word police, I started to hear faint sirens coming from a distance. Within a minute of his call, two patrol cars pulled up in front of the gate. Once the policemen stepped out of the vehicle, the guardsman told them what was going on. Debating if I should flee the scene or not, I just stood there trying to figure out how I was going to get out of this mess.

Soon after, a policeman came in my direction and asked me a few questions, like, my purpose of being there, who I was visiting, which floor I went to, why I didn't have identification. I told him exactly what I was doing and where I went. After replaying what I said to him in my head, I realized, this looks bad. I had no one I was meeting, I didn't know which floor to go on, and I didn't even know who I was going to talk to. I tried to be as polite as I could and explain how I was looking for someone to help me when a woman in a yellow jacket came from the building toward me.

Lisa was in her mid-thirties and asked me in English what seemed to be the problem. Stunned at first that she was speaking English, I quickly told her what was going on and explained that I was about to get arrested. I begged her to tell them that I was really not a criminal; I was just trying to find someone who could help me. She asked "What kind of help are you looking for at a radio station?" she asked. Trying to take deep breaths and stay calm, I told her about my search for my biological parents and that someone suggested that I come here.

It appeared that Lisa was finally getting the picture and understood my purpose for my visit. She explained everything to the guardsman and the police and requested that I be released to her. When the cops started to pull away from the gate, I started to breathe again. I don't know how many times I said thank you to Lisa, but I was just so happy she saved me that night.

Lisa asked where I lived in the U.S. and at which hotel I was staying. She then introduced herself as one of the radio station's DJs. My jaw just dropped and I was speechless. She said her home was next to my hotel and offered me a lift. I told her my story while we drove in her Hyundai Sonata.

In the car ride, I explained what I was doing there, what I

wanted to accomplish and why I wanted to return. She would interrupt with questions, wanting more details. I was happy to see she was interested in my life and my story. At one point during the car ride, Lisa started to cry. She was touched by the idea that I wanted to find my biological parents during the holidays so I could tell them that I forgive them for abandoning me. I didn't really know what to say when Lisa started tearing up.

After we pulled up to the hotel parking lot, we exchanged numbers. Before exiting the car, Lisa said she would do what she could to help, but couldn't guarantee anything until the conclusion of Chinese New Year in six days. I didn't care what was going to happen in six days, I was just relieved that I had avoided arrest, gotten a ride home and met her.

About an hour after I settled into my jammies, I got a phone call from Lisa. Her supervisor wanted to air my story the next day as a special program. Lisa instructed me to meet her outside the hotel by the parking lot at nine sharp, to do a morning radio segment.

After quite an eventful night, I spent most of my time gathering up some thoughts on what I was going to say on air. I wasn't quite sure what kind of questions Lisa was going to be asking or for how long I was going to be on air. So I took some time and looked up a few vocabulary words that I felt would be essential to know in Chinese.

Before going to bed that night, I ate the rest of the pistachios and sent out another email to my family and friends at home.

When Lisa picked me up in the morning she explained how there had been break-in at the building the prior day, which was why the guard acted so aggressively. I could understand his suspicion of a young man wandering around late at night in the elevator. I was very lucky to have met her because she wasn't supposed to be at work that night, but she was preparing the following week's program prior to her vacation.

CHAPTER 15

Why was I abandoned?

After we arrived at the radio station, I walked past the gate and gave the guardsman a wave and a good-morning smile. Happy to know that I wasn't walking into the building as a stranger, I pushed the button for the eighth floor. Soon after we arrived, a few reporters greeted me and began asking about my trip. I wasn't really expecting to answer questions from newspaper reporters, but I did my best not to be nervous and to speak clearly. As I answered questions, the newspaper people took photos of my face and of my left arm. All of the attention was somewhat intimidating, but exciting. I remembered thinking, This could be the start of something new. One of the reporters asked me a question that seemed mean-spirited: "Why are you looking for your biological parents? Are your parents in the U.S. mean?" I wasn't angry, but I was just a bit thrown off. I never did take it into consideration how people from the outside might view this story. With a very calm voice, I explained how having such a good life in the U.S. has actually enabled me to start this search.

After the newspaper interview, I had an opportunity to watch what it takes to put on a radio program. As I looked through the studio window, I watched as Lisa prepared the music and notes for the upcoming program.

Minutes before the program began, after a thumbs-up from her supervisor, Lisa waved me into the radio booth. Quickly and quietly, I took my seat behind the equipment to the left of Lisa. I was instructed to place the massive headphones on my head and to wait for the music to start. With a push of a button, my microphone was activated and the music turned off. Lisa started off the broadcast by wishing all the listeners a happy Chinese New Year, then introduced her guest for the day.

As I listened to what Lisa was saying about my story and me, I felt she interpreted my story very beautifully. Her introduction took about three minutes. I looked over in her direction and realized she was crying. I just could not believe that a total stranger I met by accident the night before was involved in my story to the point where she was in tears.

After the introduction, Lisa asked me a few simple questions. What school had I attended? What I was studying? After the simple questions were out of the way, she dove into the more difficult ones. Why did I come back? What I hope to accomplish while in Ma'anshan? I told Lisa and all the listeners of FM 92.8 that day that all I wanted to know was the truth behind my abandonment sixteen years earlier, and that I wanted to forgive my birth parents.

I wanted to know if they abandoned me because I had one arm, for financial reasons or something else. I didn't care what the answer was going to be, all I wanted to know was the truth. I wanted to know why I wasn't good enough to keep. I felt I at least deserved that. I explained to Lisa and her listeners that all I wanted to be able to do is sit across a table from my birth parents, look them in the eyes and ask that simple question, "Why did you abandon me?"

She followed up that question with, "Are you still angry at

them?" I took a deep breath, looked down at my hand and said to every listener that I was not angry at all. "I forgive them."

Trying to hold back the tears, I looked at Lisa and said thank you with a smile. My message was loud and clear, and I had the opportunity to say what I wanted to say in hopes that my birth family was listening. About half way through the program the radio station was already getting phone calls from listeners showing their support.

Listeners were leaving their names and addresses for me to contact them after the show, hoping I would join them for the holiday. They all shared their warm hearts and ensured me that I didn't have to be alone during this Chinese festival.

The idea of inviting a total stranger into their homes to spend this festival with their loved ones touched my heart tremendously. I was absolutely flabbergasted. No words could describe the feeling I felt, knowing that just days prior, I was alone with no direction.

I knew after the program that the people of Ma'anshan were truly good natured and caring.

After the program, Lisa and I were getting requests to take photos and to get my face on TV to insure the people of Ma'anshan knew my story. I was grateful at just having the opportunity to go on the radio, but I was having callers offering to put my photo and story on the Internet to ensure full coverage. Newscasts from surrounding cities wanted to air the story in case the family had moved.

No longer was I looking for a biological family alone; I had the whole city of Ma'anshan and surrounding areas talking about my story.

CHAPTER 16

Why me?

After the radio program, Lisa and I were discussing what other things we could do to maximize my time in Ma'anshan when a guest visitor I recognized showed up. I was stunned to see Mazhenjie in the hallway and asked him what he was up to. He said he was picking me up to take me to a lunch planned in my honor at nearby restaurant. I didn't really know what to say or how to react. I had no prior knowledge of this meal gathering and Lisa had just invited me out to lunch as well.

Before I could say anything, Lisa told me to go with them and that we could reschedule our lunch for dinner that night. When I got into the van, I saw some of the same people I had met at the last lunch. We were all seated inside a big room with fifteen chairs around the table and camera recording every second. Not only were some of the orphaned kids in attendance, but the head of the Welfare Institute was also there along with the woman the kids called Mother, and some new faces I didn't recognize. Other guests at the table included a few more orphanage buddies and adult leaders from the neighboring orphanage.

This lunch was in my honor. I sat to the right of the orphanage director and to the left of Cicili. I met Cicili the day before through one of my new orphanage buddies. She is quite fluent in English and had returned from Beijing to be with her family for the holidays. I sat next to her to make small conversation.

The orphanage director is actually called Mayor. His job is to protect kids in the orphanage and to make certain the Welfare Institute is well run. When I first met the gentleman, I wasn't quite sure what his responsibilities entailed or what his main contribution was to the orphanage. Until that point in time, I had never heard of an orphanage mayor. I asked him a string of questions about the orphanage and the kids that lived there. How many kids a year got adopted from the orphanage? I wanted to know.

My heart was not at all prepared to hear the numbers. Only an average of two or three kids out of thirty a year get adopted. The odds of kids older than four getting adopted are slim.

I started to get the idea that the orphanage wasn't just a place for kids to stay for a few years until they find a family. In actuality the orphanage is responsible for housing these kids for the majority of their teenage years. I asked the Mayor, "Where do the kids go if they don't have a new family?"

Children brought into the orphanage are first assigned a name, number and age. Kids who are between the ages of one month to six years live in the building that I first visited. If, however, these children aren't adopted, they remain wards of the Welfare Institute.

It so happened that I was sitting across from the woman who ran the program for older orphans. She explained the program known as Sun Village, a place where kids between the ages of seven and eighteen live with parental figures. At this point, I was intrigued with this program and asked if I could visit Sun Village. Lucky for me, they had already prepared a tour after lunch.

I had envisioned a school-like campus with large buildings,

but Sun Village was no school. It was truly a village of homes for orphaned children and house parents. Despite the graffiti and the old man at the gate, the community didn't seem too bad.

Sun Village hires parents to come and take care of these children. "Hires" sounds too strong. I should say that each set of parents is given three or four children to help raise, and given a stipend and provided with necessities such as food.

So, why does this program exist? This program teaches kids what listening to your parents means, how to respect your parents, and how to contribute to a family unit.

One family in Sun Village is provided with two rooms, one for the parents and the other for the kids. The kids are provided with bunk beds or three single beds. At Sun Village, there are a total of six families, all with access to a computer lab and kitchen. One of the last things I saw at Sun Village before leaving was the computer lab.

I was just blown away. There were more than a dozen Dell computers for the kids or families to use. Books were available on the side of the room and tables with chairs were in the middle. I could see this place was their home.

I had never in a million years ever imagined a program like this. Had I not been adopted, I likely would have been raised here. As I look back at the visit and think more about the trip to Sun Village, I'm finding myself becoming more impressed. Just think: it's a small community within a compound with your orphanage buddies living just next door. Not only that, but you are basically living your teenage life with a family. The parents that they bring in aren't just parents who stay for a month or two. These parents are in it for the long run, staying for years. And this Sun Village was not the only compound of its kind in Ma'anshan.

So, what happens after the kids turn eighteen? Unfortunately, the kids do leave Sun Village. However, these kids aren't kicked out onto the road and left to die. Each person, if possible, is provided their own room, complete with a toilet, sink and shower. They're about the size of average American college dorm room. The orphanage allows these adults to live there until they either get a good job that can support a proper home or until they get married. Mazhenjie is among those who made the transition.

After the lunch and the tour of the Sun Village, I returned to the hotel that night and called my mother in the U.S. I explained to her all that I had seen that day and the feeling of wanting to give back and to help. I asked her how I could possibly help them.

I was a college student with no money, just ideas. One of the first ideas my mom suggested was writing a book. I just laughed at that idea and said "impossible," and I know without a doubt my high school English teacher would have been laughing with me. After I apologized to mom for laughing, she gave me a few more ideas on how I could raise money for the orphanage.

She suggested I sell my story to different newspapers, magazines and other media in hopes they would spread the word about adoption in Ma'anshan. She also suggested that I write to Oprah and ask for her help. So after I got off the phone with my mom, I got on the computer and started to type an email to Oprah and Ellen DeGeneres.

I started out by telling them what I was doing in China and all the things I had done and seen. With the introduction done, I continued to explain how amazing these kids in the orphanage were for keeping such a positive attitude and not giving up. I finished the email by saying, "I just want to help these kids find families to love and parents they can call their own." It's true: from that day on, my journey was no longer just centered on me. Something great happened; my heart was with the babies and the kids who haven't been given a chance. I was no longer just searching for my biological parents, but also seeking ways in which I could help these kids find homes.

The first outing with my friends from the orphanage who never got adopted.

CHAPTER 17

Tipsy on New Year's dinner

When I arrived at my old caregiver's home for the Chinese New Year meal, I put on blue shoe covers and started to sip a hot cup of tea. The mother was sitting and chatting up a storm with me while her husband prepared the meal.

I was really impressed that the father was preparing the meal all by himself. At my home in the U.S., when my dad tries to help my mom cook, he ends up back in front of the TV watching sports. The dishes this Chinese dad was preparing looked delicious. Some I recognized and some I didn't. I was ready to dig my teeth into the sweet-and-sour spareribs.

Before the meal really started, the father opened a bottle of white liquor and poured his wife, his daughter, his soon-to-be son-in-law, his mother and me each a large glass. I started by raising my cup followed by the customary cheers and took a small sip. Boy, was I glad I took a small sip.

That particular bottle of white alcohol was hot and really strong—almost too much to handle. As the meal progressed and the members of the table kept lifting up their glasses to me, I just sipped along until my mouth was too numb to know the difference. An hour later, with a full belly and a numb mouth, I had finished the meal and was needed elsewhere that evening.

Before I could leave, though, the father and soon to be son-in-law took me down the stairs and outside to light off a few firecrackers. At first they asked me if I wanted to light the firecrackers, but I responded, "I can't afford to lose another hand." My appreciation of the firecrackers and fireworks was no doubt enhanced by the white alcohol coursing through my veins. I learned that night that family is everything during this festival. Families that live in other provinces or other cities reunite to share a meal together and to celebrate the upcoming year.

With only red scraps of paper and burnt fuses left, I gave my thanks to the family for such a wonderful meal and got in a taxi. From there, I had another dinner I was invited to by the orphan buddies back at the Welfare Institute. All I knew was someone there was cooking all the food and that it was going to be fun. I just didn't know what type of food to expect.

When I arrived just past seven that night, I walked into one of the rooms of the orphan kids to see her cooking on a hot plate. I asked her if she prepared all thirteen dishes on that single hot plate. She did, which I thought was amazing. I watched her cooking chicken, vegetables, soup, beef and other courses all on a one-pan hot plate.

As you may imagine, it was really challenging remembering everybody's name. One way I remembered them was by their physical appearance. For example, the girl who was cooking the meal had one arm and was my age and her fiancé was actually the person who was driving the van. Not too long after I arrived, the other kids started to shuffle into her room, bringing chairs and more alcohol. They took the mattresses off the beds and used the frames as tables, placing all the chairs around them. Twelve kids sat around a bed drinking white alcohol and eating amazing dishes.

It was probably one of the first times I ever felt really comfortable while in Ma'anshan. There I was, sitting with these kids, laughing, joking, crying, and I could not have felt anymore connected. These kids didn't need moms, dads, brothers or sisters to celebrate as a family. They were each other's family. I realized that day at dinner that had I not been adopted, I know I would have been in great company and would have grown up with a tremendous, supportive family.

Out of all the meals I ate with the fine people of Ma'anshan, this was by far the most meaningful. The only bad part about the celebration was the white alcohol. It was literally the same brand that I drank prior to arriving. Don't get me wrong, I'm okay with having a few drinks, but the Maotai rice wine was very hard to drink, not to mention very hot. Maybe it was the atmosphere or the rush of adrenaline, but I just took that cup and I downed the whole glass.

I never thought before going to China that I would ever get to feel what it's like to be Chinese.

CHAPTER 18

How dare you!

The fireworks were unrelenting. After hours of rolling around and yelling at the noise, I finally got some sleep. But not for long. I was awakened at eight in the morning by a reporter who wanted to take me out for a fun day with her kids. I remembered meeting her at Sun Village just days ago.

I was a little nervous, but I accepted her invitation. Her daughter and two other friends arrived at my hotel an hour or so later with a bag full of food. Before I could even say "Good morning," the reporter, Zhangyunxia, had a banana leaf peeled back and rice cakes for me. Munching and chewing, I didn't think it tasted that bad. Next came an egg prepared by her friend. Zhangyunxia said we were going to take a bus from here and visit the place where I was found abandoned and then go to the police station I had been taken. Around lunchtime we would walk to her mom's house for lunch. With the bus arriving, I paid my fare and took a seat next to Zhangyunxia. When the bus came to our stop, the five of us got out into the chilly, sunny morning. I was bundled up in my thick green jacket, but could still feel the bitter wind all over my body.

After we got off the bus, I pulled out my recorder and headphones and started to describe what I saw, smelled and felt. I was under the impression that we were going to the stadium where I was abandoned. We turned the corner and saw a large, beautiful, colorful park with kids playing in the grass and parents sitting on the benches.

I asked Zhangyunxia where the stadium was. She began to explain how, a few years earlier, the stadium was torn down and this park was put in its place. Before she could finish explaining the changes that occurred, we reached what appeared to be the center of the park and she pointed to a building: Yangjiashan Police Station.

The old soccer stadium was located in the oldest part of the city and had become neglected. I had always imagined this location would be filled with despair and poverty. Instead I saw a place filled with little kids laughing and memories being made. I saw kids running and playing with their parents; I even saw kids rollerblading around the pond. The park's main attraction was a red abstract statue at its center.

After seeing the kids having a lot of fun rollerblading, I decided to strap a set of wheels onto my feet and make a few rounds around the statue. As much fun as I was having watching the kids play catch-the-leader, I couldn't help but stop and look around to see the neighborhood. I found the nearest bench and gave my feet a break.

Sitting on the bench next to the pond, I wondered if my birth parents lived nearby. I wondered if they ever came back to visit the place they left me. At that point, I just wished that a family would come out into the open and claim me as their son. It was almost unbearable as I sat there thinking any of these middle-aged people could be them.

It was about then that I realized what this trip was becoming and doing to me. I felt so close and yet I had no leads to fulfill my quest. As I saw the kids playing and running around with their parents yelling to stay close, I got really upset. For the first time, I started to feel anger toward the biological family. I felt I had been robbed of the little things kids do with their parents as toddlers.

The more I thought about it, the more frustrated I became. Why wouldn't I be mad? I didn't get to hold Mom and Dad's hands or have a photo of me taking my first baby steps while holding onto my mom. Instead I was dumped in an orphanage. After feeling sorry for myself and finding every reason to hold a grudge, I wiped the tears away and got back on my feet. I took a couple of deep breaths and started to rollerblade a few more rounds. My ankles were getting sore as I saw from a distance Zhangyunxia waving me back to the place where I had rented the skates. Zhangyunxia said we should go to Yangjiashan Police Station before leaving.

Walking toward the police station, I was telling myself to lower my expectations and to cope with whatever they say.

Like most buildings in Ma'anshan, a gate surrounded the police station. When we stepped up to speak with the guardsman, Zhangyunxia explained to him that we were looking for a person who could help track down old records. When she finished explaining to him what we were looking for, he turned us away and said that no documents like that would be kept there.

It was a total bummer. It wasn't like I was expecting them to tell me my life's story. I was just expecting to see a copy of the police record from the March 18, 1991, abandoned child incident. I was hoping to at least learn what I was wearing that day, who reported the abandoned child. I thought that was going to be the easiest part of this journey. It turned out to be one of my biggest disappointments. I was shocked that a station would throw out records. Hadn't they ever heard of photocopying? We left the station almost as fast as it took us to get there. All I could do is keep my mouth shut and bottle up my anger to avoid a confrontation with the guard. I had already been in trouble once with a security guard.

When the family and I got back on the bus, I took a window seat and just stared outside for the duration of the ride. Time just stopped for me for a while. So much was running through my head; I was trying to assimilate what all had happened that day. The ride seemed like it was hours. I just stared out the window watching the cars pass by and the pedestrians walking with their families.

As we were in transit, I started to realize the probability of my birth family revealing their identity was unlikely. I was not looking forward to leaving Ma'anshan in a couple of days, knowing I have failed to answer the questions I had set forth to answer. I didn't know how I was going to handle getting on a plane and going back to my normal routine after all that's happened this week. Before I could pity myself anymore, my thoughts were interrupted when Zhangyunxia announced our arrival at her mom's house.

The food was great, but the people around the table were better. After we had eaten our fill, we were all ready to go home and rest from our very busy day ahead. I ended up falling asleep for a few hours back at my room when Lisa called to invite me over to dinner with her family. I looked at my watch and realized that I didn't have a gift for her parents. After getting off the phone with her, I jumped in the shower, brushed my teeth did a pit check and ran downstairs.

I flagged down a taxi and requested to stop by any convenient store to purchase cookies. The taxi driver waited while I ran in to buy a tin full of what looked like sugar cookies. He asked how my search was going. At first I was confused but then flattered that he had been listening in to my story on the radio. I told him my time was running out, but I haven't giving up yet.

After a few words of encouragement, he placed a business card in my hand. I was instructed to call him and set up a time to share a meal with his family. Blown away by this act of kindness, I smiled and said thank you. When we arrived I pulled out a ten-dollar bill for to pay him, but he refused. He turned around in his seat and cheered in Chinese, "Go, go, go!" and smiled.

Again, I couldn't believe he would invite me to his home for a meal, but then not to let me pay was just unbelievable. When I got out of the taxi, I saw Lisa standing in front of a convenience store wearing a purple sweater that went down to her knees, black boots and her hair tied up in a bun. I couldn't stop staring. I thought she looked absolutely stunning. Like my father always taught me, I complimented her on her appearance and walked with her into her parent's home.

I met both her parents, cousins and, of course, the family dog. I found it kind of funny when I saw how much Lisa resented dogs. I never did find out why she didn't like them, but she would flinch every time the dog walked toward her.

Throughout dinner, Lisa would tell me some of the encouraging words that the listeners had been posting on their fan page. Most of the comments were cute and supportive, while some were really sad.

With that afternoon going the way it did, I was starting to have doubts of whether finding my birth family was even plausible anymore, but after hearing all the encouragement from the listeners, taxi driver, I knew I had to stay with it and be patient.

Lisa drove me back to my hotel around eleven. It was weird, but I started to have this funny feeling whenever I was around her. I didn't tell her, but it was kind of that feeling you have when you—maybe—like somebody. I wasn't too embarrassed, but I found Lisa to be very attractive.

This turned out to be kind of an issue for me. Not because I'm a prude or anything, but she has a daughter. A daughter who is younger than me. She got married when she was really young, but had a divorce a couple of years ago. I didn't really know what to think about the situation, so I just tried to accept it and think about other things—and stay positive.

That night I wrote to my family and friends before going to bed to tell them about my day and how the search was going. Then it was lights out for me.

CHAPTER 19

A new day

I went outside in the cool spring air. The streets were quiet and all shops were closed so the workers could be home with their loved ones. The sidewalks were covered with burnt paper money and incense while boxes of fireworks filled the dumpsters.

It appeared the city cleanup crew had its work cut out for them until the next spring festival.

I started thinking about what happened at the Yangjiashan police station the previous day. I was still upset that important documents that should be preserved for future generations were tossed in the trash.

I was still determined and tried staying positive. So I decided to go to a different police station in hopes of a different answer. I boarded a taxi and attempted to tell the young driver that I wanted to go to a police station other than Yangjiashan. All I got was a staring blank face, followed by laughter. I must have said something wrong in Chinese. The dialect and pronunciation in Ma'anshan is very different than that of Taiwan, which is where I learned to speak Chinese. It can be very confusing at times.

For example, when I arrived in Ma'anshan, I told the taxi driver "Ma'anshan hotel please." He nodded his head and we were on our way. A few turns and an alley later we arrived at what appeared to be a brothel. The taxi driver and I used some form of charades and sign language until he finally figured out where I wanted to be driven. As we made our way through town looking for the police station, he mentioned that he heard from a friend that an American boy was looking for his birth parents.

I just looked at him and simply laughed and said, "Yah, I heard the same thing." He took a hard left and was heading into the oncoming traffic lane and then took an exit down an unpaved road rife with big potholes. Again I found myself afraid the translation got misinterpreted through the arms waving and noise making and we were going to a not so happy place.

We had, however, arrived at a police station and were in their parking lot just as I was debating to jump out. Once we arrived, I had told the taxi driver my story and that I was the American kid he had heard about. It was amusing when he turned around abruptly to judge for himself if I was really that kid. I just held up my nub and said, "Yep, it's me."

I could tell I got him really excited. He started to ask me a ton of questions. Like, have I found them yet? Are you scared? What kind of life do I have in the U.S.? He asked a bunch of questions about the search. When I told him what happened at the police station the other day, he said he was determined to help.

When the both of us entered the police station, we walked into one large room with a desk at the front. There were two officers smoking behind the desk and three others in the foyer smoking and eating peanuts. They obviously weren't too busy. The taxi driver asked one of the officers behind the desk if the records clerk was available.

The officer behind the desk said that they were not here and won't be back for several days. He was however very helpful in giving me names of others who might be of assistance. Both the taxi driver and I left leaving the station without cuffs and with some good answers. Sitting in the front seat of the taxi, I asked that he take me back to the hotel. I was so thankful for how much he helped. I wanted to give him a massive tip. Instead, he wouldn't even let me pay. That just goes to show how much love and support surrounded me.

I got back to the hotel late afternoon and decided that I still had time to run to a few more places. I got into another taxi and directed the driver to take me to the hospital. I foolishly didn't even think that Ma'anshan had more than one hospital, so when she asked which one, I was the one with the blank stare. I was thinking, "Oh, crap, I don't know." I just told her, "The nearest hospital from our current location." Turns out, Ma'anshan has four hospitals spread throughout the city. I randomly chose one of the four.

As we arrived, the hospital was nothing like I had envisioned. It was a medium brick building with metal grills protecting the windows with a small entrance. I didn't even get out of the cab at that time. I said, "Next." About ten minutes later we finally arrived at what I would call a hospital. I saw ambulances, nurses and doctors running around everywhere.

It was in the process of being renovated so the noise was quite loud. The lobby was very bright and cold and the receptionists were wrapped in their winter coats answering phones. I asked where I could find the records department for births. The girls just smiled and said they weren't open until the conclusion of the holidays. It just was not my day.

I did, however, get a phone number and address to the records building. I thought I would call them the next day and possibly catch someone in the office. I told the nurses what I was looking for and asked if this was the right place. The nurse and receptionist were quite optimistic.

When I started to walk outside, I heard a commotion. A mother screamed and cried hysterically as nurses carried off the woman's young child on a gurney. Trying to respect their space, I stepped aside and let them pass. As they passed, another gentleman put firecrackers in the path of the gurney and lit them off to pay respect to the deceased. Even though I didn't know who they were, it was still very difficult seeing first hand a family member of a loved one passed away on a gurney. If anything, it made me miss my mom and dad in the U.S.

I walked away—and kept walking—until the sound of the mother's tears became softer and softer. It wasn't dark yet, so I decided to explore the neighborhood. Not too far from the hospital, I had come across a night market that had just opened for the evening. Even though I didn't buy frog legs or eat a scorpion, I was content with my strawberries on a stick.

I went to the nearest KFC for dinner, and then took a taxi back to the hotel to Skype with my mom and dad in the Sates.

The police officer who assisted me in finding the family that found me.

CHAPTER 20

What's next?

Now that it was the weekend of the biggest holiday of the year, I really didn't expect to accomplish much. I spent one day traveling around Ma'anshan sightseeing. I got up early that morning and got in a cab. Instructing the driver to take me in the middle of city, I went from there to window shop. It was so weird seeing these streets bare. What had been hundreds of people were now only a few unfortunate homeless people. Lucky for me, McDonald's was open and I was able to get my Big Mac fill for the day. Because space is so often limited in larger Asian cities, buildings tend to be built upwards and not outwards. It was really neat sitting on the third floor of McDonald's and eating a burger. When I was finishing my last bite, I pulled out my phone and decided to call Cicili. In case you forgot, Cicili is the one I met through my orphan buddy who returned from Beijing to be with her family. She also went with me to Sun Village.

I called Cicili and asked her what she was doing that weekend. When she answered, I asked if she could join me at McDonald's to help plan my last few days in Ma'anshan. I felt really bad for asking, but she did tell me to contact her if I needed any help. Did this count then? I clenched my teeth as I asked her, thinking I would be rebuffed. Instead, she said she could meet in half an hour.

I was pretty excited that she was willing to step away from her family activities to help me out. When she got there around 2, I bought her a McFlurry and we went to the third floor to jot down some ideas.

I decided to return to the Yangjiashan police station and the orphanage for supplementary information about my DOB and medical records.

With a plan set, Cicili went back to her home and I continued to walk around the city. Not too much later, I got in a taxi and met with Lisa at a coffee shop. She was wearing a red dress, black pants and a gold necklace with her hair down. When she asked if I wanted to meet her for coffee, I told myself to stay cool, act professional and to be on my best behavior.

When she asked if I liked coffee, I just assumed we could go to Starbucks. I could not believe what I heard next. Ma'anshan did not have a Starbucks. Lisa tried to explain how people in Ma'anshan prefer to drink tea over coffee, so there are more teahouses than coffee shops. So, what I thought was a coffee meeting turned out to me getting green tea.

We had a nice conversation. We talked about her daughter and her plans for the future. We discussed about her aspirations and how she got into the radio business. It was just a very light simple conversation. It was honestly just us reflecting upon our lives and how we got to where we are today. I learned that Lisa has a very interesting past and has become a stronger woman because of it.

As I was sitting across from her in the booth, I just could not stop staring at her eyes and her smile. She had by far one of the biggest smiles I had ever seen. After coffee, Lisa was kind enough to drop me off on her way home. I was tired and just as I got cozy in the bed, my phone rang with a call from Mazhenjie to have dinner with him and a couple of other people. Saying no wasn't an option. Mazhenjie was waiting for me in the hotel lobby.

When I came downstairs, the grin on his face was priceless. He smiled as if he had somehow tricked me. He's a fireplug of a man, standing about three feet tall and solidly built, but it's his beaming smile that defines him. As we weaved from bicycle to bicycle with carts filled with tofu on way to the night market, we finally arrived at the hotpot restaurant. A hotpot is a pot with broth that is on a burner. As it simmers, you slowly add vegetables, meats, and seafood into the pot until soft and tender. The concept is simple and the taste is absolutely amazing. I was met by more than a dozen older kids from the orphanage who had been saving us a spot.

Since Mazhenjie and I were last to arrive, we made our way to the frozen food buffet line to choose our fish, squid, beef, shrimp, and vegetables to add to the pot. I later learned that the restaurant makes a really small profit from customers buying a hot pot. However, the restaurant draws most of their revenue from the liter-size beer bottles they sell for fifty cents. Our table of seven drank over twenty-five bottles of beer. By the end of the meal we had some really happy and sleepy Asians. Some rolled and some crawled out of the restaurant that night.

I managed to send my family and friends an email that evening. Whether it made much sense or not is a different story. I awoke the next morning with a massive headache. Despite the hangover, I was happy for the night out with those kids.

Everybody was relaxed and having a good time.

What I thought to be just a routine Sunday turned out to be the complete opposite. In fact, I never want to relive that morning. I got a call from Mazhenjie the next morning telling me that he was coming to pick me up. He didn't tell me what we were going to do; he just said I would enjoy it. I would be at his mercy, once again.

We arrived at what appeared to be a multi-floor restaurant. We walked through the rotating doors and put on a pair of slippers, and then we were escorted down a hall. I took a left and then BAM! We entered a locker room with a bunch of old naked men.

I wanted to run for the exit immediately, but Mazhenjie grabbed my hand and pulled me toward the hot springs. He cupped some water in his hand and said in English, "Good." I looked at him and said, "Naked."

All I knew for sure at that moment was that I was not getting into that hot tub in a birthday suit with a bunch of naked guys. I was very adamant about this and very upfront with Mazhenjie. It became even more challenging to get my words straight as he was standing in his birthday suit not too far away.

So after further discussion, a Speedo was brought out for me to wear. You know in those Jackie Chan movies with all the oversized business guys sitting in a sauna smoking and spitting, well it was that and then me in my Speedo. Needless to say I stuck out like a sore thumb.

I was glad to move to the next section of the treatment, water massage. It was very interesting to say the least; the guy wrapped his towel in the form of his hand and then used hot water to relax muscles. I was in heaven for those thirty minutes, but it got even better when my brothers handed me a pair of shorts and shirt to change into after I took a shower. After leaving the hot springs room, three young women escorted us together into a large room where we would start the final leg of our spa visit. First came a back massage and then moisturizing mask was applied to our faces while the girls worked on our feet. I looked at Mazhenjie and nodded my head in approval.

The next two hours were a blur, I just remember getting a two-hour massage and eating fruit the entire time while watching TV. When finished, we hung out in the building playing on the computers, shooting pool and of course playing ping-pong.

From what I learned, you basically rent out those rooms for the day. So, we had arrived there around eleven and didn't leave until seven. If we weren't in the lounge area, then we were back in our room chilling on our beds watching TV or eating food.

When Mazhenjie went up to the counter to return his slippers, I saw he pulled out a credit card. Before I could fight for the bill, it was paid. I asked Mazhenjie how often he came to the spa and he said at least once a week, sometimes more. With this most soothing day almost over, the only thing left was to brag to my friends and family how much I had been spoiled that day.

That night I couldn't help but think how amazing this experience has been so far and how rewarding it had been to meet all these people. Never in a million years did I ever expect to find what I had already found. Never did I think I was going to socialize with kids who have the same past as me. Just to be able to meet these people and see how well they turned out was inspiring.

At that moment I felt truly ashamed for the way I had looked at my life in the U.S. I had taken so much for granted. I felt somewhat ashamed that it had taken me sixteen years to truly understand how blessed I was to be provided a second chance. Until that day, I didn't think I would ever see life in the same way. This trip was originally a search for my biological parents, but ended up being a search inside myself and my soul. I wanted to give something back, to do something that was bigger than me. I wanted to make a difference for these children. I announced to my family that I was going to do something for these kids some way, somehow. It was just a matter of finding out how and when.

Presenting flowers to the family that found me that cold winter morning and took me to the police station.

CHAPTER 21

You saved me!!

That following Monday morning, shops were beginning to open, people were back at work and students back to their studies. The Mayor of the orphanage picked me up to find some birth records. Once we arrived at his office, one of the first things I noticed was how organized his filing system was. The folders were separated by year and then into smaller books of kids' profiles.

Once we found the folder marked 1995, we had to spend some time looking through all the photos and profiles for the kids adopted during that year. After finding my photo we discovered some very basic information such as name, sex, weight, and height.

This particular profile provided a special number, 58. We opened another cabinet and found a folder with that number. It was a large tan envelope that had been sealed for some time. After giving it a nice dusting, I opened the envelope and poured the contents out on the desk: five photos and a packet of papers. Of course, the first things I looked at were the photos. They were photos that my U.S. parents had sent the orphanage after I was settled in the U.S. My father was in a photo, my sister and I took a bath in another, and there were some other photos where I was in my Halloween costume.

The packet of papers was the next thing I took a peek at. It was about ten pages thick and very formally put together as a book. A lot of the documents were just certificates of authentication and others were just copies of my birth certificate.

I even saw my parents' signatures on what looked like a contract. I'm sure the contract had a "no return policy." I did, however, come across a very odd small sheet of paper with beautiful handwriting. Once I took a good look through the packet, I asked if I could copy all the documents. I was shot down as fast as if I had just asked to marry his daughter. I was confused to what the big deal was with photocopying, but I just got a nod in disapproval. I never did get a straight answer, so I took the last few minutes to write some things down and to take a few pictures of the documents before we exited together.

I left there with just a little information, not exactly what I was hoping for, but it was still something. I had a very odd feeling in my gut that I was missing something from that packet. He appeared nervous and I couldn't figure why he was so tense.

Later that afternoon, Cicili, some reporters and I went to the records office that the hospital nurses had recommended. We decided to go into the office to see if the secretary or anyone else was available to assist us.

Once we located the office of birth documents, we all got ready to go in. The cameras rolled on my hand preparing to open the door. I anxiously turned the door knob, hoping to make a grand entrance. Talk about a letdown; the office was closed for lunch. We found a couple of phone numbers on a whiteboard hanging next to the door. We figured they had to be someone important. So we gave the first number a ring, just to hear them say, "Call the next number on the board." So we called the other number just to hear them say, "You're in the wrong place." This was proving to be another dead end, but this time with a contingent of newspeople documenting my failure. The reporters suggested we go back to the Yangjiashan Police Station. Before we got in their van, I told them that I had already been there and came out empty handed. They still wanted to go, so Cicili and I got in the van.

When they pulled off the road and parked, I didn't recognize where we were. It had appeared we entered through the back of the station. Going through a small alley, we found the back door of the police station that led to stairs. We figured that the upper floors would be more administration and record-keeping.

I told them before going in that if this was another dead end, I just wanted to call it a day. With the camera rolling, I led the group up the stairs to the second floor. When we exited the staircase, there were three doors on our left. It was a dark hallway with the only light coming through the one window.

Seeing that the first door on the left was cracked open, I knocked on the door. A gentleman with short black hair, heavy police-issued jacket, and sunflower seeds at his desk called us in. I introduced myself and gave him the quick story and my intentions in his office. After seeing the film crew, he told them to get out, but let one stay after arguing with one of reporters.

We all took a seat on his couch with tea in our hands and I began to tell my story from the beginning. He was a bit dazzled by the unusual request, but after realizing the sincerity in my voice, his demeanor softened. He first asked what legal documents I had from the orphanage and if I had useful leads thus far. Sadly, it took me two seconds to give him the sheet of paper and to respond with a "No." I figured I was facing another dead end, so I might as well ask a few questions. I was curious what the process was when a baby is found abandoned and turned in. Before he answered my questions he wanted to let me know the records department in the bureau was nothing to brag about. Everything back from the early 1990s was kept in boxes. Shortly after he finished his speech, I heard him call out someone's name.

The officer had a records clerk come into the office and explain their current condition and whether or not I was likely to find anything meaningful. It was about this time when another uniformed officer came in with a big blue book opened up on a page.

The officer showed me the book of "receipts" of children being found that year. He explained that, once a child is found, the person who brought the child to the station must fill out one of these forms. The receipt was for an infant boy found at the stadium on March 18, 1991. That had to be me! It was very basic information: names, addresses, location found and date. But it was information—a name.

The person who found me was a He Wenyiu. Everybody in the office was really excited to finally hear a name. The challenging part was trying to put a face to her name. The officer and his assistant were kind enough to search the database. Three results came onto the screen. The first was very unlikely due to her age. She would have only been five at the time. The second person was also unlikely due to her physical address being in a different province of China.

Then we looked at the last person with the name. We clicked on her profile and it showed exactly what we wanted to see. Approximately six years ago her home address would put her parallel to Ma'anshan stadium. We had finally found the lady who was responsible for taking me to the police station and saving my life.

After doing some more research, we were saddened to hear "He Wenyiu" had passed away in March 7, 2005. With a heavy heart and just a black and white photo on the screen, I said a simple thank you and prayer. When we all started to quiet down, the officer made a few phone calls to the family in hopes of passing my story along to them. Unfortunately, all numbers once connected to her or her husband have been re-assigned to different people. The officer did come up with an idea in hopes of finding another name with a number, so he quickly sent the records clerk girl to fetch another document.

She returned with a book that was already opened. We were able to contact the woman's son and verify that his mother was the one who turned in a baby in March 1991. After the officer hung up the phone, he handed me a piece of paper with an address and phone number. He said "they would like to see you tonight if possible."

Before arriving at their home, I went to a flower shop to pick out some flowers. Then, the entourage of news reporters and I went house hunting for Building 20. Once we found the building we buzzed Room 991. When we got out of the elevator, a boy no older than 10 greeted us with shoe covers. After the addition of a few more reporters, we filled his kitchen with flashes and questions. I took a seat next to the grandfather of the household, who was probably in his mid-eighties.

The grandfather had been a factory laborer and his now deceased wife had worked in a restaurant. I asked him a bunch a questions regarding that particular day, but it took some time for him to remember specific details. I asked him if his wife had been alone when she found me. "Or were you guys together?" He answered without hesitation, and said, "We were walking as a family."

The grandfather said that they found me in a basket wearing red clothes and wrapped in a blanket. He then went on to say that when they first looked at me they thought I was such a beautiful baby and were confused why I would be abandoned.

It turned out He Wenyiu didn't know I had one arm until arriving at Yangjiashan Police Station. He laughed and said, "It was very strange how we found you. You were wrapped in a blanket kitty-cornered in an alley." He said they observed many people passing by the basket and not one person acknowledged it or stopped to look at it.

The mother went over to see what was in the basket, expecting it to be nothing but maybe some bread or fruit. She was very surprised to see a beautiful baby quietly sleeping there. Not a tear was shed or a yelp, from what I was told. The son, whom I guessed was about age forty-five, couldn't remember if there was a piece of paper on me or not. He said there may have been a piece of paper with my birthday written on it, but he couldn't be sure.

After countless photos and questions from the newspeople, I made sure they knew how much I appreciated their willingness to help a baby in need. One of the last things the grandfather told me was, "If we hadn't already had three kids and weren't struggling to get by, we would have kept you as one of our own." I think at that time, everyone in the room was silent and in awe of this sweet old man and his wife's legacy.

When all the data collecting was completed and all the resources tapped out, I was happy to have found the family that saved my life that day. I was happy to be able to shake the father's hand and say thank you. I felt we accomplished a lot more than what I ever expected. It just shows with hard work, perseverance and a little help, anything was possible.

CHAPTER 22

Second-to-last day

I woke early the next morning to get ready for my last radio broadcast. I typed up my thank-you speech for the people of Ma'anshan and sent it to Lisa to translate. Lisa and I planned to meet before the broadcast for our hour segment. For the first half-hour, we took phone calls from the listeners who had some words of wisdom. The listeners knew it was my last day and that I had not yet found my biological parents.

The first caller was a retired mother who had followed my progress. She offered to provide a shelter and food should I need accommodations. She mentioned it's important to have a mother figure while in China, so if I was to need anything I wasn't to hesitate to call her.

Another caller was a gentleman with a taxi company that wanted to take me out to lunch. Unfortunately I was not free that day to eat with him, but he requested I join him and his colleagues for a special lunch in my honor the next day. I was informed from Lisa that I was to be receiving a special gift at that lunch.

Flattered by the invitation, I happily planned my next day's lunch with him and his friends. I was instructed to meet him outside my hotel at noon. I now had the chance to give my thank-you speech to all those who have helped me this past week and half. The hardest part about giving that speech was knowing it would never be enough to just say thank you for their support and generosity.

I read out loud the letter of thanks I had written, trying not to cry or stumble on any words. Midway through the letter I was out of breath. It was by far one of the hardest things I have ever had to do. Thankfully I was able to finish the letter and say goodbye for the last time.

After the program, I answered a few more questions and took a few more photos with Lisa behind the microphone. A reporter at one point asked me if I was going to be upset if I didn't find my biological family by the time I left. I looked him and responded with a "No," because at that point I had already found the family that cared and nurtured me for the first four years of my life and that was something to smile about and something I could be happy with.

When I exited the radio station for the last time, there was a large group of people cheering and yelling my name. There was even one lady who ran up and gave me flowers. I was so touched I couldn't help but start to tear up. It was absolutely unbelievable the amount of people who cared for me and followed my story.

Lisa's boss took us to lunch at a really beautiful restaurant. Lisa and I sat next to one another, trying to figure out what our plans were going to be for the last two days. After the lunch we set up an interview area in the restaurant for me to personally express my gratitude toward those who helped me on my quest. I spent a few hours that afternoon hanging out and talking with Mazhenjie, trying to figure out what would be next for him in his life. He said he would focus on growing his company. Before I left to have dinner with Lisa and her friends, Mazhenjie asked if

I wanted to spend my last night at his place.

Doing so was kind of poetic; I had spent my last night in the orphanage before being taken to the U.S. I would now spend my last night in this city at the orphanage once more before returning to my Oregon home.

CHAPTER 23

My last day

It was snowing when I awoke the morning of my last day in Ma'anshan. I bundled up and rushed off to "People's Republic Ma'anshan Hospital" to meet a reporter.

This reporter had called me the previous night to ask if I had done a DNA search in hopes of finding a family member or relative. I figured what better way to start off the day then getting blood drawn for a DNA test.

I was about midway to the hospital when I got a phone call from the reporter. The People's Republic Hospital does not have the proper equipment to do a DNA test. The reporter was, however, very optimistic and provided another hospital that had the proper equipment, but it was located two hours away in Hefei, Anhui. I had plans throughout the day and people to say goodbye to.

So I decided against the DNA test and continued with my original plans. After choosing not to go to Hefei, I had the taxi driver take me to The Ma'anshan Daily to meet with the reporter.

The reporter brought me inside and offered a cup of warm tea. He then handed me a copy of the newspaper. There I was,

wearing a cheesy smile beneath my fat baby cheeks on the cover
of the paper. He asked me to read the paper and tell him what
I thought of the article. I just looked at him and said, "I wish I
could."

It was about this time when another reporter from a
Guangzhou newspaper came into his office to ask a few questions.
He liked my responses to his questions, but clearly wanted
me to disclose something that hadn't already been printed or
broadcasted. He asked for some stories of my childhood and
for my favorite teenage memories growing up in the U.S. After
pouring my heart out on the table of my favorite childhood
memories for an hour, I gave him a copy of our family Christmas
photo for the newspaper.

My last day was a whirlwind. I rushed from the Ma'anshan
Daily office to the taxi company owner who had invited me to
lunch during the radio interview.

There were about fourteen people waiting in a banquet room.
We all took our seats. With Lisa to my left and a famous artist
to my right, we started eating the dumplings, chicken legs, ribs:
another menagerie of great Chinese food. Everyone at the table
expressed kind words of support. Several said "Welcome home."
I had heard that a lot on this journey, but those words resonated
on my final day. This did feel like home.

I lifted my glass of orange juice to all of them and said, "I'm
happy to have another place I can call home."

After lunch, we arrived at the orphanage and the leader
escorted us into a conference room where we were all served
tea. While we were mingling and talking, the leader introduced
a lady to me.

This lady apparently was assigned to me as a child and saw
to it that I stayed healthy and well fed. It was really a fantastic
moment when I showed her the photos my grandfather took
from their visit. In one, I'm being comforted and hugged by her.
It was really cool. I didn't even recognize her from the photos;

she no longer had bug-eyed glasses and long hair. I guess I've changed too: I got just a little taller and lost my fat baby cheeks.

I was curious to ask her about my overall behavior as a child. She said I was a really smart and beautiful baby. She said I didn't like to talk or communicate with the boy babies as much as the girl babies. I, of course, found this to be no surprise.

Two cups of tea later, we all got back into our respective vehicles to make our way to an art museum. We entered through two through beautiful stained glass doors. The place was packed and filled with beautiful, intricately designed works and plants. We met one artist who took us to his studio, which was next to the museum.

It was here when I finally had the chance to see my piece of art. It was a rabbit. The animal has special meaning for all the people in China. It was the year of the rabbit for the Chinese and it is the year I came to Ma'anshan.

Next on my schedule was to take Lisa out to coffee to thank her for everything she had done. When we were in her car I saw a puzzled look on her face. I asked if we were lost and she just giggled and said no. But we were. Lisa had apparently taken one left too many and we found ourselves leaving the city limits. After joking for a minute or two about her driving skills, I was waiting for Lisa to turn the car around to head back into town. About five minutes and a phone call to her friend later, Lisa was able to get a basic understanding of our current position. While some would think that getting lost is a bad thing, I enjoyed seeing all parts of the city.

Their countryside isn't majestic scenes of flowing wheat fields or rice fields. A majority of it appeared to be abandoned buildings with trash-filled lots. I imagine in the turn of the century, a huge number of farmers and families moved into the city for better jobs and opportunities.

After we got back on track, Lisa dropped me off at KFC, where I ran in and purchased four buckets of chicken, drinks, apple pies, corn sticks and boxes of shrimp chips for my orphanage friends. It was my way to show gratitude for their warmth and help. When Mazhenjie and I finished eating the chicken wings and shrimp chips, we had to make an early exit to visit his uncle, a calligraphy artist, to pick up my gift and my parents' gift.

When I saw the artwork, I was speechless, it was beautiful and the strokes were so intriguing. He gave my parents a five foot long scroll with what appears to be a poem. I have yet to understand the full meaning of the scroll. I was given a traditional Chinese fan: one side translates to American Chinese representative and the other, nature of wind and a smooth journey.

It is a very beautiful fan with gold leaves imprinted into the tan canvas. When I said my thank-yous and goodbyes, Mazhenjie went to the KTV to meet up with the others, but I still had a few more stops to make before I could meet them.

I met He Li Juan at a McDonald's, the first person I met at the airport, to say goodbye. It was sad leaving such a sweet girl, but we exchanged hugs and went our separate ways.

I didn't have much time to feel bad. I knew I had to find another taxi to take me to Lisa's house to pick up my luggage. Because I had checked out of my hotel that morning, I had left my bag with Lisa in her car, and was going to grab it when I said goodbye to her that night.

Finding a taxi in the city center when it was thirty degrees outside was near impossible. I found myself running about half a mile trying to flag down a taxi. My legs were tired and I was exhausted, but, finally, one stopped. I told the driver the address and then closed my eyes. Just as I was getting warm and starting to feel my fingers again, I arrived at Lisa's apartment. I ran up all five flights of stairs and knocked on her door. With my bag sitting right by the door, she invited me inside. Realizing that I was late in meeting the orphanage buddies, I took Lisa by the hand and said, "Thank you for everything."

With that smile of hers, she didn't say anything. With the

strap on my shoulder, I gave her a big hug and proceeded down the stairs.

As I stood outside waiting for the taxi, I couldn't help but stare up at her window. I doubted that I would ever see her again. The only things I could do were think about her and pray that she finds someone who makes her happy.

Now that I was on my way to meet with my orphan buddies, I was getting excited to hear everyone sing KTV. KTV, or Karaoke TV, is a form of entertainment very popular with Chinese people. It has become part of their culture. KTV rooms are all over the city, providing food, drinks and great music all through the day and night.

Well, I should retract the comment about "great music." When I sang "Lucky" by Britney Spears, I'm certain it was unfortunate for those listening.

We had a great time and after about three hours we headed to the orphanage for a good night's sleep. I was in my room getting ready to go to bed, when I heard a knock on the door. Wondering who was still awake at midnight, I slowly popped my head out to take a peek.

Mazhenjie couldn't sleep, so he wanted to go to the spa and was wondering if I wanted to accompany him. Kind of confused why he didn't just drink a cup of warm milk or read a book to help him fall asleep, I figure it was better not to ask. So we hit the spa and stayed there until eight the next morning.

When we got back to the orphanage, there wasn't much time for farewells. I had a plane to catch. As I said my departing words from the airport to all my friends and new family, I reassured them this wasn't really goodbye, but more like Take care and I will see you soon.

So, I left on February 11, 2011, without knowing the identity of my biological parents. Was I upset? I may not have found my biological parents, but I found my people. The trip also reinforced what I had always known: I have great parents and a great family in America—even if we're not linked genetically. The family I ended up finding wasn't the family that birthed me. What I found was right under my nose the entire time. I didn't need cameras or the radio to find them: all I had to do was get in a taxi and walk through those gates at the orphanage. The truth is, I did succeed in Ma'anshan. I found a family there. I found my brothers and sisters.

My first minutes with the family after reuniting in the airport.

CHAPTER 24

Could it really be true?

On February 18, 2011, a mother bought a newspaper that would soon change her life. There, in front of her, was a picture of the infant son she had abandoned so long ago. With two children by her side, the woman hurried to meet the reporter who wrote the story. "He's my son," the woman said, pointing to the picture in the newspaper. I am told she was overcome with emotion as she stood in the newspaper lobby. Bibo, the reporter in charge of my story, told the woman that I had already left. Bibo sent me an email with the news in hopes I would respond immediately.

I was back in Taiwan and had just left my dorm about that afternoon to meet my friend in a city south of Taipei. This trip was supposed to be relaxing and a chance to get out of Taipei before school started in a few days. I was riding on a bus when I pulled the phone out of my coat pocket and scrolled over the email entitled good news... your biological mother came to the newspaper. I opened the email and started translating. It took me about thirty seconds for the impact of the news to hit. I was stunned and wanted to make sure I had properly translated the email, so I unbuckled and turned to ask the person who was sitting behind me to read it back to me. I laughed and cried at the same time, overwhelmed by the news that the woman who gave birth to me had come forward.

I immediately dialed the first number that came to mind, my real mother. Not paying any attention to the time difference, I woke my parents at one in the morning to tell them the good news. I found myself laughing the entire phone conversation with them. I could not believe the search for my biological family may have finally come to fruition.

When I got off the phone, I sat back and took one long deep breath. With all the mental mayhem going on, I failed to see two unread messages from the same reporter. I once again scrolled over the email and, with a push of a button, I was beginning to read the new message. However, there was not any text for me to read.

I scrolled down a little and saw a photo of a boy said to be my biological brother. I was breathless. Here I was sitting on the bus, one moment just rocking out to some Trace Adkins country top hits when I got this email saying "Your family came forward," and just minutes later, seeing my blood brother. Nothing in the world could have prepared me for those moments on the bus.

Staring at his photo, I could see resemblance immediately. The first thing I noticed was his chin. It was pointy just like mine. I couldn't believe how much our bone structure looked alike, our noses, eyebrows, and nice teeth. The next photo emailed to me was of my biological sister. She was wearing a pink jacket and was on the phone next to a computer. The first thing I said to myself was, "Oh God, what is it with me having sisters addicted to cell phones?" It was the same story; she had the same bone structure as I did. In the photo she was sitting down, so couldn't tell how tall she was.

The next photo I saw was with the mother and uncle standing side by side. There was a caption next to the photo saying he was the uncle--not the father. The mother was wearing her brown leather jacket with black pants and her hair in a ponytail. I guessed she was in her late forties. The uncle was wearing a dark blue vest with a dark shirt underneath.

For the next twenty minutes I just stared at the three photos, scrolling back and forth between them, studying the faces, the smiles. I wanted to hold onto that moment of joy as long as possible.

When I finished looking at the photos, I opened the second email from Bibo, which described the family and provided ages. I had two siblings and a set of parents to go with it. My brother was age twenty-two and my sister age 18. That made me the middle child.

When I arrived in the city where I was meeting my friend, I just gave her a big hug and explained why everybody on the bus hated me.

A happy reunion between a mother and her biological son.

CHAPTER 25

Mom…?

With everything that happened that day, I couldn't sleep very well. I spent a majority of the night sitting in bed watching infomercials and glancing at the family's faces on my cell phone. I did manage a few hours of sleep and when I woke, I checked my cell phone for new messages. It appeared Bibo hadn't wasted any time in sending me emails. I sat in my Christmas boxers and stared at the phone screen. "They really want to talk to talk to you. Call them immediately." Also Bibo wrote, "The mother would like you to address her as 'Mother' or 'Aunt.'"

I knew at that moment, and without hesitation, that I would never call her mother and I would still feel very uncomfortable calling her aunt. My real aunts in America are very special to me and so it didn't feel right to bestow that title on a woman that was a stranger. I was a little concerned how she was going to react to my stubbornness.

It was about this time I started to get duplicate emails urging me to call them immediately so they could hear my voice. I was feeling kind of irritated and cornered after the first few emails hailing my attention. My response was somewhat guarded. I wanted proof that these people were blood kin, perhaps a DNA test. I didn't want to get duped nor have my hopes dashed by a mistake. I was relieved to hear they were willing to take a DNA test on Monday and send me the results here in Taiwan. I decided to call Bibo to express my feelings more directly than what my email seemed to be doing. I said, "I believe in my heart they are my biological family. I am truly looking forward to meeting them soon and to giving them a hug. However, I need to make sure I'm protected and my emotions are not being twisted."

I simply asked Bibo to express my feelings and to tell the family. If the family was willing to be patient through this process, then I would be more than happy to answer any question they may have in person later next week. In his response Bibo wrote that the family would be patient, understood my caution and looked forward to my visit in the near future.

Bibo organized a phone call with the family and gave me reassurance they weren't going to push me to do anything rash. I still felt I needed my voice to be heard. What neither the family nor Bibo knew was that I went to the travel agency and applied for a visa to reenter China. I knew that if I waited till next week for the DNA results it would take another two to three weeks to return to Ma'anshan. Because I felt in my heart that they were who they said they were, I decided to take a gamble. If this proved to be a hoax or a case of mistaken identity, I would be out two hundred for the plane flight, and worse yet, I would be back to square one. Preparing for a phone call like this proved to be a little challenging. I was questioning my ability to communicate with the family and decided that I should ask a friend of mine to help translate should I need assistance. The accent in Ma'anshan can be difficult to understand, especially if you're talking over the phone. Also, the family would be excited and likely speak at high speed. So I asked Frances Lee if she would join me during the phone call.

I dialed the number given to me by Bibo. After a few rings a female voice answered on the other side. This was not the old scratchy voice I was expecting to hear. I had dialed the sister's cell phone.

When I introduced myself, she was very excited and I could tell she had anxiously looked forward to my phone call. When we both got over the shock of hearing each other, I asked to speak to her mother. Without much of a conversation, she gave me her mom's cell phone number, which I promptly dialed after saying goodbye.

That scratchy voice I was expecting to hear had answered the phone. When I introduced myself, I didn't hear the reaction I was anticipating. It was a calm voice and a quiet hello. Not a response you think you would get after twenty years. The conversation with the mother was very brief.

It was really weird because all I heard that day and the day before was how much the parents wanted to talk to me. So, I figure when I actually did call, I would have at least been answering some questions. But, she didn't ask me a single question. I don't know if it was because she was shy, scared or something else, but I was basically talking to myself during those two minutes.

Next on the call came the uncle. I felt less nervous with him.

I had only prepared one question for him: "What are the parents' occupations?" The uncle explained that the mother works on their rice patty field and the father is a shoe cleaner. I did not know if he owned a shoe cleaning company or what his job entailed. The uncle explained further that the father is in

Hangzhou, another province, working in a shoe factory.

Once I heard what their jobs were, I couldn't help but ask when my actual birthday was and in what year. It seemed the family wasn't at all ready for this question because they spent countless minutes talking in the background about dates. The mother admitted she was not good at remembering dates due to her illiteracy.

I think I heard three different possible years I could have been born. She couldn't remember what calendar system she had used to note the birthdate, which I found disappointing. The mother thought about it a little more and there was some conversation in the background. The uncle then told me that I have no birth records because I was not born in a hospital. A midwife helped my mother give birth on the 20th of December in 1990.

When I heard my exact date of birth being confirmed, I compared the dates from birth to abandoned date. I came to the conclusion that the mother had kept me for four months, which means she must have given me a name. What was it? They responded with a most unexpected and ruthless answer. They didn't name me. How can you have a baby for four months and not even give it a name? I was outraged, but didn't express my anger over the phone. Was I that inconvenient, that unwanted, not even to be given a name?

I ended the phone call feeling upset and depressed. However with everything that was said on the phone, we did establish a plan. That following Monday the father would do his DNA test and send his results directly to Taiwan. On that same day, I too would be doing a DNA test. It was now just a waiting game, eight days of waiting, patiently hoping this was finally the end of the search.

CHAPTER 26

DNA results

It had been eighteen days since the search for my biological parents started. With the support of my friends and family both in the U.S. and China, I am happy to announce that my quest had ended. On March 1, 2011 in the late afternoon, I had in my hand the envelope.

As I was sitting in Dr. David Chang's clinic, I wondered before opening it, What will this change? How will the feeling of closure and finally being able to find the truth feel? Will I be scared to meet them or will I even feel anything at all?

So with Dr. Chang staring at the envelope, I peeled off the adhesive tape and removed the document. With my heart beating faster and faster and my hand shaking, I pulled out the yellow sheet and read the report. It was the first time in my life I ever wanted to read or hear The test is positive from a doctor.

Leading up to that day wasn't as easy as going into the bathroom and giving my mouth a good swabbing for DNA. In the course of the two weeks, I first had to understand the rules and laws between China and Taiwan for paternal testing. Soon after calling and visiting every hospital in Taipei, I was left with no choice but to ask for the father to send his DNA in the mail.

Thinking that it was a simple if odd request for the father to send a couple of Q-tips of his DNA to Taipei, we ran into some other unforeseen issues, including skepticism toward DNA testing.

With all these factors playing a big roll, the family requested having a doctor swab for the DNA and taking it from there. There was however another problem for the family. They had to drive two hours to find the nearest hospital with the proper equipment to do the DNA test. So the Wu family hopped in a van and went to Guangzhou. Once the swabbing was over, I received a phone call reporting the success in the procedure and it was my turn.

When I finally felt we were moving in the right direction, I was slapped in the face by the law. It appears DNA testing between these two countries cannot be officially recognized if the two parties aren't physically next to each other during the test. With this said and every other rule, we were able to find a loophole: We could do the test in our respective countries and then have one of the party members fax over the results from their country.

Dr. Cheng in Taiwan compared my test results to the father's, proclaiming a 99.97% chance of accuracy of a DNA match. I called my parents that night to tell them the good news. I think they too believed deep down that the search was over the moment they saw photos of the sister and brother. But, it was still nice to have a DNA test to confirm everything. After I told my parents the good news, they asked, "Now what?" I said, "Well, I have my visa now; I can buy the plane ticket now, tomorrow or never."

Both mom and dad responded with a "Good!" and instructed me to put the flight on their credit card. Because I always listen and do what my parents tell me to do, I did what they said and purchased the flight that night on their credit card.

That was a very difficult conversation to have with them. I was basically telling them, "I'm going to go visit my biological parents." It was really weird for me to say that and I'm sure it was strange for them to hear.

My mom sent me two emails that epitomize her unconditional love of me.

We love you soooo much. Please remember to pray before you make each decision. I think it will help. Even if you don't find all the answers you are looking for, you have found so much to be blessed about. We are blessed to have you and thankful for all the days you have been in our lives. Love you more. MOM

Just a cute little story and a little perspective. We got your picture on my 30th birthday and we got you nine months later. Margie took your picture to school for sharing and showed everyone her new brother. We discussed how we could turn Ma WuBao into a name that would start with the same sound—so we have Wyatt (although Grandma Rosemary wanted us to name you Wyath). You were named! We referred to you as that name immediately. Love you more. MOM

My parents, family, and friends all shared concerns about my emotional state during this crescendo. They all wanted to know how I was feeling inside and out. I told them this wasn't the same kind of nerves I had when I had my first kiss, but it wasn't the same scary feeling I had when I watched a horror movie either. I was feeling kind of relaxed. I knew what I was about to do, and all I could do is pray for strength and keep my head up.

Even though I wasn't scared, I did have a few concerns. I was a little worried how the family was going to handle my stubbornness in not calling the parents "mom" or "dad." I was also afraid that the family was expecting more than what I had to offer, that being friendship. I couldn't help but wonder if the family would be apologetic or just relieved that I turned out the way I did.

I was concerned that the family might have different motives in mind and I would be totally oblivious. With all these worries in the back of my mind, I knew I had come too far to turn around or take the easy way out. I was, however, truly afraid that if I didn't take this opportunity to meet them, I might never find that closure I was looking for.

When all was said and done, I wanted to look back at my time in Ma'anshan and not feel the way I did the day they abandoned me. Before I left for China, I had some time to ponder these things. I am just a college student, I'm not rich; the only thing I could offer the family was my friendship and forgiveness.

I could only wish one thing for the family, and that was a sense of alleviation. Whether the family dumped me because of birth defect or for financial issues, I wanted them to understand that I would forgive them for what they did that day, forgive them for not caring enough to give me a name, forgive them for not trying, but most importantly forgive them for not giving me a chance to be a part of their family.

I couldn't even begin to fathom what was going on inside both the biological parents' and kids' minds at that point. I didn't know if the kids were excited to meet me. I didn't even know if they knew about my birth at all. Within thirty-six hours I would find out. When I started this quest, I imagined this trip was about me and only me and my thirst for knowledge. I now had to take into consideration how the family felt about this discovery.

What kind of emotional toll is it taking on them? They're probably as conflicted as me, and nervous about our meeting. And then what happens next? Will we stay in touch after I return to the U.S.? Will the parents write me emails or will the siblings tweet me? All these things lingered in my mind, as I was about to take this next step.

As the days got closer, this step didn't seem like a leap anymore. It was just another day in the park. Sure I might have puddles in my path, but I could either jump over the puddle or just walk around. Either way, I was ready to take this head on. Let's do it, I said to myself.

Just a small part of the welcome party that embraced my return.

CHAPTER 27

The day

The day started off like any other morning but would end like no other. Trying to be as quiet as I could without waking up my roommate, I put some last-minute things into my bag and made my way out the door to catch a taxi.

While riding in the cab to the airport I still found myself wondering what my first words were going to be once I saw the parents in the terminal. I decided not to rehearse, but to just let it happen as naturally as possible.

When the pilot announced that we were starting our descent and to fasten our seatbelts, that's when it hit me; I was just thirty minutes away from fulfilling a dream.

I buckled myself in tight and closed my eyes and prayed all would go well and that I would get through this in one piece.

While the plane was taxing to an available gate at the Nanjing Airport in Anhui, I quickly snagged my hair comb and my toothbrush from my bag so I could look and smell fresh. What appeared to be a normal landing didn't seem so normal to me. The seatbelt light was no longer illuminated and the plane was parked at the terminal.

People stood, as always, the second the light went out and started to gather their carry-on bags. The only thing left was for the stewardess to open the door and for everybody to make a mad dash for the exit. Being familiar with customs, I had no issues going through. The only thing left was going through the gate where the guests would await my arrival. I couldn't do it. I was breathing irregularly and sweating through my cardigan sweater. All that was left separating me from the family was the declaration line, a simple line that had me place my bag through a metal detector. A retractable wall screen was the only thing keeping me from seeing the family on the other side. I could hear them say, "I see Ma WuBao; I see Ma WuBao."

I wasn't ready. I went to the bathroom. Not literally, but I stood in front of the mirror telling myself to toughen up. I splashed some water on my face and re-applied deodorant. After brushing my teeth and then my hair, I was looking and smelling more presentable.

I think the guy who was at the urinal right next to me was wondering what my problem was; he just kept staring at me giving me weird looks. After a few minutes of psyching myself up, I grabbed my backpack, did a pit sniff and a snot check and left the bathroom.

I was greeted by more than thirty reporters and random spectators. Trying to find Lisa, I finally spotted her in the crowd wearing her yellow jacket, and made my way toward her direction with open arms. As Lisa was coming toward me a little Asian woman pushed through the photographers and placed herself between Lisa and me.

I recognized her from the photos. The mother, my biological mom, was hugging me and squeezing my arm. With cameras rolling and clicking the only thing I could do was embrace her. As the mother was hugging me, she started to cry. I pulled out a tissue from my pocket and helped her dry up the tears. After I told her, "Don't cry. Everything is okay," she started to cry even more. As the reporters were taking photos, they were all asking how I felt or whether I was happy to be back. Honestly, at that point, I was speaking, but I didn't know what I was saying. I was walking toward people, but didn't feel my feet moving. My heart wanted to be happy, but I didn't know how I felt. All I could do was stare out into the crowd and try to remain poised.

After a few minutes of consoling the mother, I saw a man weaving in and out of the reporters. With the mom attached to me, I could see that this man, about five foot six and in his mid-forties, was the biological father. I didn't know if I should hug him or shake his hand, but he pulled me in and gave me a really big hug.

Not exactly knowing what else to say, I just said "Hao Jiu Bu Jian," which means Long time no see. He laughed and then proceeded to give me another hug. It was a very happy moment for both of us. Seeing a grown man cry told me a lot about how the father was feeling at that time. After we exchanged hugs, he rolled up my sleeve to review the nub. He was analyzing its size and growth. I wasn't sure what to think about that, but I just let it happen. A few minutes later, I felt a tap on my left shoulder.

My older brother is about an inch or two shorter than me and was having trouble composing himself. It didn't take long for me to see how much he cared for me and how happy he was to see me after all these years. I'm not sure why, but I felt very comfortable around him. I respectfully called him "older brother," and stood back and took a long look at him from toe to head. I was just amazed that I was standing in front of my biological brother; it seemed like a fairy tale.

I gave him one more hug and then rubbed his head like I do to some of my closer friends and said, "All right!" I had one more sibling to search for.

When I took a quick glance around and asked "Where's Mei Mei?" "Mei mei" means younger sister. It was then that part of the crowd split, and at the end was my younger sister in her pink jacket, blue jeans and retro shoes holding a little girl's hand. The sister ran over to me and gave me a warm and gentle hug.

When the hugs were all exchanged and tears were falling to the floor, a large crowd had formed, so we moved everybody outside of the airport to talk and answer some more questions from reporters. I found it very amusing and intimidating how tightly the mother was holding onto my arm as were we walking.

After we got outside, I answered a few more questions when I started to see more people I recognized, including taxi drivers, Zhangyunxia, and some people from the radio station.

It was such an exciting moment for me and all those who participated in my search. When I took a deep breath and looked at all the faces in the crowd, you could just see and feel the joy of a job well done. When I got done hugging and shaking hands with the friends I met from my last trip, it was time to make our way toward the taxi caravan.

Unfortunately it wasn't as easy as opening the door and sitting. Before we could leave, we had some disagreements to where we were going. With the commotion of the cameras, reporters and recorders surrounding us catching our every word, I no longer had any control. The mother's death grip kept me from leaving her side.

I called out for Lisa's assistance, but unfortunately my voice was lost in the crowd. It was about then that I started to feel scared and overwhelmed. I no longer felt in control. With my frustration level rising and my patience wearing thin, I shouted,

"Stop!" I pulled away from the mother and went to look for Lisa in the crowd. I was happy to see her at the edge of the circle, looking for me.

I explained to Lisa we needed to get control of this situation and tell them what we planned before arriving. The plan was quite simple: we would go to the hotel together to check in and then have our private conversation with the family before we did anything else.

I had to say something to silence the crowd. So with another deep breath, I once again said, "Stop!" Suddenly, the family stopped pushing me to their car and it was quiet enough for Lisa to speak.

Lisa explained that we would go to the family's home in Dangtu after we spoke at the hotel. Sadly, the family wanted to hear nothing of it and basically told Lisa to shut up. At that point, I was feeling miserable and frustrated. I had had it. I was prepared to just get back on the plane and pretend none of this ever happened.

I looked at the family and told them that I am not happy at all and that I would not be going anywhere but to the hotel. Apparently looking them in the eye and using my Chinese really made a point. With the father pulling the mother away from me, I signaled for the brother to join me in the one-hour taxi ride to the hotel.

This picture represents a bright future and a new bond, and shows that I am taller than the older brother.

CHAPTER 28

The truth

The taxi ride from Nanjing airport to the hotel was one for the books. Lisa sat in the front seat, her co-worker was to my left and the brother was on my right. Just as we pulled onto the highway, the brother turned to me and asked his very first question. "Little brother, are you hungry?"

I just said, "No, I'm fine, thanks." Nodding his head with approval, he smiled in my direction and asked if I was cold. Again, I responded with, "No, I'm fine, thanks." For the first ten minutes of the car ride, he kept asking me these kinds of questions. I could tell all he wanted was to make me comfortable. I shifted the conversation by asking him a flurry of questions. He told me about school, jobs, music and even girls. Without even thinking, I assumed that the brother took classes of some sort. I first asked if he was in college, but he said no. I then asked when he graduated from high school; he didn't. I must say, I was a little shocked to hear that he did not complete high school. I wasn't quite sure how to respond.

I wasn't disappointed in the brother or sister for not completing high school; it was just surprising. In America we just assume most people at least attended high school. I thought that I, too, might not have completed my studies had I not been adopted. The awkward silence was broken when the brother asked about my musical taste. Not quite sure how to answer his question, I started naming off country artists I enjoy listening to in the U.S., Garth Brooks, Trace Adkins, Rascal Flatts, Tim McGraw, and Alan Jackson among them.

As I was naming off these artists, I could see the puzzled look in his face wondering who I was talking about. Seeing that he didn't understand the names of the artist, I started to sing a few verses in hope he would understand the beat of the music. Nothing, absolutely nothing but laughs from all the passengers; I thought I hit the high notes pretty well, but apparently it was just free entertainment for them.

I asked the brother when he first learned about my birth. I didn't know what to expect. The brother said he was made aware of my birth from a very young age. So this was as big a moment for him as it was for me.

It seemed only natural that I ask about his relationship status. It turned out that he was engaged and his fiancée was at the airport as well. I just didn't see her. From what I understood, they planned to marry soon. It only seemed right to ask if he had any cute single ladies that he could introduce me to while I was there. Sadly all the ladies he knew were married, dating or not desperate enough.

What I remember the most about the car ride was how sincere the brother was with me. It wasn't just an act for the media. He helped carry my backpack, helped with my seatbelt and, of course, made sure I wasn't hungry. We were quickly forming a bond.

I literally could feel the love, compassion, warmth that would be expected within a family. There was no doubt about it; he truly embraced his role as the older brother.

There was one point during the taxi ride just before we entered Ma'anshan that he started to cry. I could tell by the look in his eyes it was tears of joy. He was crying because this was a dream come true for him, too. I put my arm around the brother and just patted his head. With the convoy of taxis still behind us, we pulled up in front of the hotel lobby. When the door opened, the brother stepped out first and I quickly followed. With the reporters filling the lobby, Lisa and I proceeded to check in. I was very fortunate to have a room prepared ahead of time at no cost to me. Now with the key in hand, a long trail of people made their way to my room.

When we got into the room, the first thing I did was give the family the present I prepared ahead of time. I gave them chocolate bars, sugar canes, jelly and some photos. I had printed them the night before and they included family moments, friends, sports, prom photos, my ex-girlfriend and my dog.

When I gave the family the present, I realized that there were reporters standing on my bed. I almost wanted to chew them out for their lack of manners, but was too busy listening to what the family was saying. About five minutes after we entered my man cave, I heard a reporter asking to start the cleaning process.

The cleaning process? I must have misheard what was said. Minutes later, Lisa and the mother emerged from the bathroom with a washcloth and proceeded to wash my face. Cameras flashed and rolled, recording the bizarre ritual. I could feel the gentle touches as the mother went from ear to ear and to my chin. I could see in her eyes what this ceremony meant for her and her family. I later learned that the cleansing ceremony is used when a member of a family returns home after being gone a long period of time. The cleansing removes the dirt accumulated from traveling.

After the mother softly patted my face with the cloth, she then proceeded to my right hand and finishing with my left nub. I really don't understand the fascination the parents had about my nub. But when the mom was cleaning the nub, she stared and manipulated the arm in different forms. She started to whimper and then cry.

I took the very rag she used and wiped her tears away. With that, she started to cheer up. I showed her how I could make my nub look like a smiley face. So whenever I'm sad or lonely, I bring out my buddy that never leaves my side.

The sideshow was complete and reporters left the room—finally. Now I could focus on why I was really there. This was the moment I had always dreamed of, the moment where I would learn the truth about my abandonment, the day I would learn if the family tried to care for me. It was time for closure.

Sitting in front of the very place I was born and called my home for three months.

CHAPTER 29

No choice

The mother, father, brother, sister, Lisa and Victor remained with me as the last reporter left my room. Victor is Lisa's longtime friend who stayed to help me translate the conversation. I needed to make sure the family understood my questions and that I understood their answers.

In the room, there were two chairs with a table between them, next to the window. Victor and I sat in those chairs. The mother and sister were sitting on the bed directly in front of me and the father was sitting on the bed off to the side. I assumed the brother was too anxious to sit as he stood next to his mom, holding her hand. Lisa sat on the opposite side of the room trying to respect our space but still near in case I needed support.

The first thing I wanted to get out on the table was how happy I was for them to come forward and what it meant. I told them, "You didn't have to come out, but you did, and for that I thank you." I continued by saying what this conversation meant to my family and me. I was at a loss for words in the beginning of the conversation. I did my best to show my gratitude, but I still wonder to this day if I could have done or said something more.

I looked both the mother and father in the eyes and said, "The answers you give me will not at all hinder our relationship. I just want to hear the truth and if you tell me the truth, it will only make our relationship stronger for the years to come." With a nod from the father and just tears from the mother, I asked my first question.

"Why did you leave on March 18, 1991, at the stadium?"

This question has always been the sole real reason why I started this search. This was the question I needed answered more than anything else. I wanted to know if they left me that day because of my deformed arm. I was prepared to hear yes, but hoped in my heart that wasn't the case.

The father took the lead on answering without pause. The father told us about the family's desperate financial situation twenty years ago. They were very poor and their home was not suitable to raise children. He was working ten hours a day as a laborer and could barely afford enough food to feed a family of three at that time. Adding another mouth would be impossible. During the three months I lived in their home they fed me, took care of me and kept me alive. Despite how hard the dad worked to bring in more money for the family, they were out of options.

So in February of 1991, I was wrapped in warm clothes and taken to a nearby village to be given a second chance. It was at this point in his story that the father started to cry. He went on to explain how after they left me in the village it took a matter of minutes for them to regret their decision. They quickly returned to take me back home.

After another month, the reality of being dirt poor set in again. The family did not have enough food to sustain itself and I was requiring more. They were concerned about my health and development—and that of their other children. Tears rolled down the father's face as he continued the story. I too was emotionally vexed and at a complete loss of words.

On March 18, 1991, the father and mother did what no parent would ever want to do once, let alone twice in one year. So using a basket as a crib and layers of clothes to keep me warm on that cold morning, the family went to Ma'anshan, where there was a new factory that provided good wages and safe work.

Not knowing any better place to leave me, they placed the basket in front of the factory entrance, hoping that some worker with a well-paying job would rescue me. The family watched from a distance as countless people simply walked by the basket. Finally, a woman and a family approached the basket and promptly took it to the authorities. The father held back the mother who lurched as the strangers carried me off. As fate would have it, I ended up in the Ma'anshan Welfare Institute for the next three years.

The second question, "Did you know I was at the Ma'anshan Welfare Institute?"

I wondered if the biological family ever cared enough to find me. Again, the father was the first to speak and replied with a "Yes."

When he said yes, it wasn't a happy chirpy yes; it was more of tone of disappointment, embarrassment. The father, with his head down, continued to tell his story just like it happened.

Later that year, with a touch of mercy from God, the father was able to get a better-paying job at a factory, the very factory adjacent to the place I was left. The job didn't just bring long days and harder work for the father, but it also brought pain. The pain caused by looking out onto the very courtyard where he left his child still played fresh in his mind as he passed by.

A few years after they abandoned me, it appeared the family's life was coming together. One day after work, the father went to a family's house in Ma'anshan to share a meal. With a full belly and a back full of pain from working, the father left the house and passed by the Ma'anshan Welfare Institute. He stared at the gate, wondering whether to enter or not. Then he took the long walk through the Institute's courtyard in hopes of seeing a familiar face. Even though it was a few years later, he just had to look for the best-looking boy with one arm.

In the corner of the courtyard was his flesh and blood. A son he had not seen for three years was now taller and walking freely. When he approached the lonely boy playing, he introduced himself and started to play with me, but did not mention the fact that he was my dad. About an hour passed when a caregiver came over to talk with the father and ask what his purpose was that day. Not knowing what to say at that moment, he made up a story explaining his brother and sister in-law were planning to adopt. After the caregiver heard his story, the father was directed to go to a governmental building to provide documents proving the child would be their first.

Quickly leaving the grounds with new information, the father reported the news to one of his younger relatives who had not yet had a child. What followed proved to be a tough month of debating whether or not adopting was right for them. Now with the family wanting to adopt me, the three of them went to the orphanage one afternoon to start the process.

Between pauses, I would see and hear the mother whimper and cry as she relived that horrific day. The brother's face was red from crying and the sister was staring at me with happy tears falling from her left cheek.

During the process of debating and trying to get all the adoption paperwork done, the father would periodically visit the orphanage to keep me company. When it appeared that they were ready to move to the next stage, the father, aunt and uncle all went to the orphanage to make the official request.

When they arrived at the institution they looked for me in the courtyard and in the bedrooms. I was gone, not to be found or heard. A caregiver told my father that a baby girl and I had just been adopted and were taken to the U.S. Since that day the father has never returned to the orphanage.

Seconds after running down a dirt road for two minutes.

CHAPTER 30

Welcome home!

A deal was a deal; after the family answered my questions, I agreed to go to their home later that evening. As I was putting on my seatbelt in the van, the mother looked at me and instructed me to change into warmer clothes. I told her that I was perfectly content with the clothes I was wearing.

Not only did she demand that I change, she also demanded that she and the brother escort me back to my room to ensure I put on enough layers. From a white clear sack, the mother pulled out black long johns, a heavy wool sweater and a pair of winter socks. I exited the bathroom five pounds heavier and sweaty.

I took my seat in the back between the mother and brother. It was a really awkward car ride for me. Even though I felt really close to the brother, I had nothing to say to the mother. Maybe it was because I was nervous to speak in Chinese with them, but I pretended to sleep all through the car ride to avoid the awkward silence and blank stares.

A tap on my shoulder from the brother woke me up from my pretend-sleep announcing our arrival. With the car still in motion, the brother was asking me if I wanted to run. I laughed and said, "What? I didn't bring running shoes, and why do you want to run?"

He replied, "We won't run too far; we will just run to our home from the road, just like we would if we were little kids playing." Starting to understand the picture, I did a few stretches in the car to avoid hurting my delicate body.

I had no idea where we were. It was in the countryside and trees didn't have leaves on them. It was kind of quiet, with houses spread alongside a road. The last McDonald's or KFC I saw was about twenty miles back. It's really hard to explain exactly what I saw, but I think Paranormal Activity was filmed here.

When the van finally came to a complete stop, about twenty people surrounded us. When I stepped out of the van, people were grabbing my hand and shaking it madly up and down, saying, "Welcome home! Hello! Hello!"

For the first five minutes I stood on the side of the road meeting extended family members. If you asked me today who they were or what their names were, I couldn't tell you.

After I shook the last hand, the brother asked if I was ready to run. Before I even answered, he took his place on the line and waited for me to do the same. The sister joined us, too. The road we ran down wasn't the road we arrived on. It was even more remote. The family was scattered along the road cheering for us to start. I motioned to the brother to start running and he sprinted away. I just laughed and stayed in my spot and then chased after him. As I was running, fireworks and sparklers were going off on the side of the road, some soaring hundreds of feet.

The brother has quite a set of legs on him. Had I not tried to push him over while running, I'm sure he would have beaten me. As the three of us returned to the family's house, I could see that the cheering crowd had swollen to more than one hundred people. Many were still lighting off fireworks, sparklers and firecrackers. Before we got to the crowd, the brother handed me a lighter and a roll of firecrackers. He said I was supposed to throw it and let the roll unravel.

I was more than a little nervous about holding a ten-pound roll of firecrackers. And, I wasn't certain whether the fuse was lit. So, I quickly chucked the roll, which, as it turned out, wasn't lit. The brother picked up the pack of fireworks and handed it to me again. When the last firecracker in the roll popped, we continued our trek toward the crowd ahead. As we got closer, the crowd started to rush the three of us. Hands were coming from all directions wanting to shake mine. People were standing on their stoop smiling and waving, kids were running around screaming and making loud noises. Dogs were jumping and barking, adding to the chaos.

Many of these strangers stared in amazement, commenting on how much I resembled the brother. I waded through the handshakes and cheers toward the family's house, anxious to get inside and escape the growing crowd. There was one lady with arms the size of my mom's but a grip as deadly as my dad's. She pushed her way through the crowd and placed herself right in front of my view. She grabbed my hand and squeezed it so hard it went numb.

The brother reached in between the people and pulled me out. He said he wanted me to see something—the house I was born in.

Some people might call the building a shack, at least by American standards. The house was split into three sections. Before moving into their new home in 2009, the brother and sister lived in the right portion, sharing a room. The middle room was a kitchen/dining room/living room and the left side was the parent's room. Each of the three rooms was tiny, about the size of my college dorm room. An outhouse in the yard served as the bathroom. The house looked like it had been abandoned and left to rot. The ceiling was large pieces of plywood thatched with some kind of grass or hay, and the floor was made of concrete. It felt like the room could collapse at any moment. With the crowd of people following close behind, I stepped into the very room I was born in. I couldn't believe it; this was my birthplace. I was humbled and thankful at the same time. I looked at Lisa to my right and smiled. When the crowd got silent, a reporter asked me how it felt to be back in this room.

This return to Dangtu taught me how lucky I am to live in the U.S. Seeing where I was born and how modestly these fine Chinese people live gave me a greater appreciation for my great parents and lifestyle back in Oregon. As I stood on the concrete floor I thought of my bedroom back home and my queen-sized bed. My birth family shared an outhouse; back home I had my own bathroom. I felt ashamed at how I took all that for granted. I have since realized that a home isn't defined by having a couch, TV, bathrooms and beds. Home is family. And for these poor people, my birth people, this shack was their home for more than forty years.

After what seemed like hours in their old house, we left the vacant building and went to the family's new home, where there were three big tables and a bunch of food awaiting our arrival. Sitting at the main table with me was the brother on my left, the dad on the right and across from me was the uncle. With a raised glass of rice wine, a toast was made and then we started eating. Dish after dish was brought out to our table, and people were just surrounding the table as we were eating watching our every move. After about an hour, I had my fill of chicken legs, beef and duck.

After the meal, the brother and sister, her boyfriend, his

girlfriend, Lisa and I went to Karaoke TV to sing some songs. I didn't know what would happen at KTV, I just thought it would be a fun—a family outing of sorts. To both Lisa and the family's surprise, I even sang some Chinese songs. That night, I learned singing talent does not run deep in the family.

Our night had only begun. We all loaded into the car and made our way to the massage parlor. After arriving at the very massage parlor I had been to multiple times already, I started wondering just how commonplace spas were here.

When we got our massages, the five of us were in one large room with a massive TV in the middle. As the American kid I am, I focused more on the TV than the tea and biscuits being served.

It was late and I was tired, so the family decided to call it a night. We would all meet at Lisa's radio station the next morning. I had a king-size bed waiting for me at the hotel.

Matching jaw bone structure.

CHAPTER 31

On the air

The sister and dad were first at the radio station with a McDonald's breakfast in hand for me. We all chatted between bites until Lisa came to into the lobby to prep us for the show. She was very insistent that it was okay if I started to cry or needed to take a break. I reassured her that I would be fine and would get through it. After a nice introduction of the parents and me, Lisa started off the show with a question for the parents. "How does having 'Ma WuBao' back in your life feel? After a very sweet answer from the dad, I had the pleasure of hearing the mom's feelings about my return.

With the easy question out of the way, Lisa then asked what every listener of FM 92.8 was likely wondering: "Why did you abandon your baby?" I knew it was an inevitable question that was going to be asked and I felt that listeners should know. They were there from the beginning with me, invested emotionally in my story. And, they had been very supportive. Everybody in the studio cried while the father retold the story. The mother sobbed too and left the studio. I was impressed by the father's courage and blunt honesty. When the father finished his time on air, it was time for the brother to come into the studio to talk about his feelings and emotions. Lisa asked him what it felt like to have his brother come back. He just said he was very grateful to my American parents for allowing me to make the journey.

What the listeners didn't know was how much the brother's reaction affected the father who became so overcome with emotion that he, too, exited the studio. As the brother kept giving his answers, he was looking directly at me and speaking to me—not just the listeners.

In the next segment we took phone calls from listeners. One of my favorite callers was a middle-aged woman who had followed my story from the beginning and so generously offered me shelter should I return anytime soon. Before I could say thank you, she cut me off and offered accommodations for my U.S. parents should they want to visit Ma'anshan.

As soon as the show ended, I scooted my chair away from the microphone and gave Lisa a big hug and said, "Thank you for everything you have done." I then gave the brother a hug and told him how much I appreciated him. Before I could do anything else, I used the bathroom to wash my face to hide any evidence of tears. Now that the difficult part was out of the way, the family and I left the radio station with renewed hearts.

CHAPTER 32

Thank you

Who would we be if we didn't pay a special visit to the people who cared for me so long? My biological family and I both agreed that we owed everything to them for what they did for me in my first four years. But, how do you thank them and all who supported you? It would be like thanking your parents for raising and feeding you. I concluded that the best way—the most sincere way—to thank a parent is never to take them for granted. Embrace their love and keep them in your heart.

Still feeling that wasn't enough, the family and I marched into the orphanage with boxes of fruit. It was a well-accepted gift and we were happy to give them the present. It dawned on me the moment I first went to the orphanage that these caregivers never leave. Their dedication is inspiring. I had always envisioned the orphanage as a slum or some dark, sullen place. In fact, where I stayed was a well-run place with top-notch workers

I knew this was probably the last time I would get to see the kids. So I separated from the group and went back to see the babies for a while. I really was going to miss seeing their cute smiles and strange looks. The only thing I wanted to do was to walk around the room and to see all those beautiful faces one last time. After walking around for while saying goodbye to these kids, I saw my favorite buddy sitting in his crib getting ready to start the day. I helped him put on his sweater and socks. He was spunky and tugged on the camera attached to a small strap around my neck. The little boy reminded me of what I was probably like at that age. He was curious about everything, talkative, funny and, of course, handsome. I just hoped that he, along with all the other kids, would have a home to call his own by the time I returned.

After about half an hour, I started to see some familiar faces enter the nursery. The family and some reporters got their chance to see these kids first-hand. I loved seeing how the brother turned all soft when he talked with the kids. It was a side of him I had never seen before. I could see this was difficult for the mother to see firsthand.

Saying goodbye to all these kids was a really sad moment. Their fates were undetermined and I could only pray that these kids would find a home soon. A person like, myself, who once lived there can only wonder, Why was it me who got chosen? After we all said our goodbyes to the children, our entourage gathered outside in the courtyard. While standing there, I heard an older gentleman yell my name. Having no idea who he was, I just turned around and waved to the stranger. He yelled my name once more and motioned for me to join him. As I was walking, he told me to hurry up. A bit offended by his manners, I began jogging toward him.

The old man was distressed about my lack of memory. He started telling me stories from when I was very young. Apparently I was his little buddy while at the orphanage and the man was quite happy to see me return taller and bigger.

We were all getting pretty cold standing in the courtyard, so we all went into a conference room at the orphanage where

I got to say my final thanks and write a letter. A few younger ladies entered the room, causing a stir. I had no idea who they were or what the commotion was all about. Like the gentleman my father taught me to be, I stood and waited for introductions. Apparently these ladies had been on the staff that took care of me at the orphanage. After we took a few photos, I gave the Mayor a handshake and said thank you for everything. I didn't get a chance to say goodbye to Mazhenjie, so I had a packet of photos and a letter I asked the Mayor to pass on to him. Getting in the taxi and exiting the compound was quite a sad moment. I tried not to look back, but I couldn't help but wonder when my next return would be.

I tried to hold onto that moment for as long as I could, but a reporter asked me to pull out the letter I wrote, interrupting my thoughts. Speaking into a microphone, I read it aloud. The letter I wrote was going to be played on TV with pictures of the orphaned kids. It thanked the radio station and audience for all the help, generosity and kind words. I couldn't have thought of a better way to say goodbye and thank you.

When we left the orphanage, we didn't have too much more planned. All I wanted was to get to know them on a more personal basis. So, when we got back to their village of Dangtu, the first thing I asked to see was where the mother worked for the majority of the year.

With my brother and sister, we took the path on the side of their house leading out to the field. The field seemed like it went on forever and there was no end to the rows of rice. Families living in that section of the city each receive a plot to farm. It's not enough land to farm commercially, so families primarily grow crops for themselves or sell small amounts. My family had one quadrant about five minutes from their house. I believe the family's field is about 50 x 25 feet of rice field. After feeling the leaves with my bare hand, I plucked a stem and asked how much the family makes per year off its crop. It amounted to a couple of thousand dollars a season. I could only think about how hard these people work for so little. Yet, they seemed content and even proud.

The best chicken soup I have ever had.

CHAPTER 33

My first goodbye

On Sunday morning I missed four phone calls from my siblings and had two unread text messages. The two text messages were from the father, saying "We are here." The next thing I knew, I heard a couple of knocks on the door. I was seconds away from throwing my cell phone at the door while hiding under the covers. I threw a stick of gum in my mouth and did a quick mirror check before receiving my first guest of the morning.

With no Starbucks or Dutch Bros. in Ma'anshan, I was happy to at least see Mei Mei, with a black coffee and a bag of cinnamon twists in her hands from KFC. She said to hurry up and that she would meet me in the lobby. Quickly trying to get dressed and eat my twist was not an easy task in its own. After a few umphs and tugs I had five layers of shirts on and three layers of pants on. Feeling that I would be warm enough for the day, I wobbled down the tenth-floor hallway to find the elevator. In the lobby of the hotel, I met my sister, her boyfriend and Lisa.

With some coffee still left in my cup and just a bag of cinnamon in the bottom of my bag, the four of us loaded the car and proceeded to leave town. Before leaving town we stopped at a shoe store. I was thinking maybe Mei Mei or her boyfriend wanted to pick up a pair of sneakers before leaving town for Ge Ge (the brother)'s celebration, I figured it was no big deal.

The four of us walked into the store and Mei Mei turned to look at me and said, "You pick out shoes." Feeling flattered at that time and shy to accept the offer, I smiled politely and refused. I knew I didn't want the family to buy me anything, but Mei Mei insisted that I pick out something. My newfound sister then started to grab shoes off the rack.

I could see how happy the sister was to help me pick out the right pair of Converse high tops. She asked if they were too tight or too small, and she even laced them up for me. With my new pair of shoes sitting in my lap, the journey to the countryside continued.

While in the car heading to Dangtu, Mei Mei asked if I would stay my last night in Ma'anshan at their home. Of course when she asked me this question, she referred the house as mine as well. Still feeling quite adamant about keeping my personal space and having a place at night I could just unload was still very important to me. With a minor joke in Chinese about the shoes being a bribe, I said I would think about it.

I turned to my left and asked Lisa what she would do if she were me in this situation. She sighed and said to me, "Your birth mother has been asking me the past two days to convince you. It would mean so much to your birth mother if you were home for the last night."

Looking at the new pair of shoes in my lap, then looking up, I told the sister the bribe worked and I was more than happy to stay at their home for the last night. Before I even finished my sentence, she was on the phone with the mother telling her the exciting news. On the topic of news, today was a very special day for my older brother and his fiancée.

Today was their engagement party, where they would be with both sides of the family enjoying a menagerie of wonderful dishes. Pulling up to the house, you could already see the party had started and people were getting tipsy—and it wasn't even noon. With a few hellos and introduction of the bride-to-be family members, Lisa and I took our seats for lunch. About thirty seconds after we sat down, I heard a yelp from a dog and a scream from Lisa. Trying not to laugh too loud to avoid causing a scene, I quickly pulled the cute white puppy out from under the table and showed Lisa the cute face. Unlike every other girl, Lisa wasn't drooling over the cute puppy eyes or the shaggy white hair. Apparently, she doesn't like dogs because of an unfortunate encounter. Nevertheless, I slipped the pup a few treats under the table, much to Lisa's chagrin.

After the meal, Lisa and I took a really nice walk. We saw some really nice houses and abandoned homes. Most families heated or cooked with wood-burning stoves and had bundles of sticks and kindling stacked in their yards. With the permission of another family, I stepped inside one of their kitchens and looked at how they kept the fire going. With one person cooking at the stove, the other would be sitting close to the ground feeding and poking the fire to keep it nice and hot. After a little bit of convincing, their grandma allowed me to feed the fire while they were finishing up a dish. When you have a fire like this, you really need to be close down to the ground. After minutes of bending over and putting sticks in the fire, I was burning up. I don't think that saying "If you can't handle the heat, then get out of the kitchen" could have been more true.

During our walk, I saw contraptions on top of the houses. They looked like solar panels of some sort, but had a bunch of PVC pipe running off them. I later learned that each house has a solar water heater on its roof. It was the last thing I ever thought I would see on top of their homes in the middle of nowhere.

It's quite an interesting contraption. The heater is a long cylindrical tube resting on four legs strategically placed where it would receive the most sun. From the water cylinder there were solar panel tubes absorbing the sun's rays, thus providing hot water for all to enjoy. After a little stroll and enjoying each other company for an hour, we turned back toward the house to celebrate some more.

When we got back to the house, the brother appeared to be waiting for us. Talking faster than ever, he seemed panicked. "You're late. We need to go!" It just seemed to be the story of my life that day. I was apparently late again for something I had no idea I was doing.

Our car carried us down the dirt road and then turned onto a hard-surface road. After about a six mile drive we pulled up to a rock mining facility. We walked through knee-high weeds and came up on a gravesite. One of the uncles had arrived ahead of us and was stooped cleaning off the tombstone and preparing to burn paper money.

When the cement pad was brushed off, the brother knelt down in front of the tombstone and motioned to me to join him. This was his grandfather's grave—my grandfather. As I knelt beside him, the only thing I could do was mimic what he was doing. After the brother bowed a few times, the father handed us a large stack of paper money to start stacking.

Carefully laying down the yellow squares of paper onto one another was very difficult with the wind blowing. After covering the cement pad that rested before the stone, the uncle handed me the lighter and asked if I would light the pile of money.

Very touched by his request, I took the lighter.

As the flames got bigger and the stack got smaller, the brother and I placed more and more yellow squares onto the burning pile until there was nothing but ash and a charcoal residue left.

With the stack of paper burning on the grandfather's cement pad, the brother went into great detail explaining what the writing on the tombstone meant. He explained how each mark on the tombstone represented how many kids he had and then how many grandchildren.

Once the brother explained who each grandchild was and which tally was his or hers, the brother just stopped and became motionless. After a few seconds without blinking or saying a word, the father softly said, "Don't worry about it." There was no mark for me on the tombstone.

All I could do was comfort the brother and to let him know it was understandable why I didn't have my own tally. But the truth was that I was feeling conflicted. The weird thing is, I shouldn't be sad. I wasn't in the grandfather's life. I think that's what upset me the most was the idea of them not recognizing my birth and just forgetting me entirely.

We returned to the car and continued down the road, pulling off into a grass pasture. It was muddy and the weeds surrounding us were taller than the car. There were no other cars in sight. We drove along a bumpy, muddy road until we pulled up to what appeared to be a building the size of a barn.

When we got out of the car, we still had some walking to do. I did my best to avoid stepping in the fresh mud. The mother went up ahead and knocked on the front door. A lady who had to have been in her eighties came out with a cane.

The mother and father greeted the lady with a warm bow and a smile and thanked her for her time. The brother was standing next to me throwing rocks and I was trying to figure out who this elderly person was. After a few minutes of conversation between the mother and the lady, the elderly lady motioned me in.

With a gulp, I took a deep breath and followed her inside.

Within seconds on being inside this room, you could tell she was some medicine doctor or shaman. Incense permeated the air and jars of herbs and other plants filled the shelves. She pointed to a seat and I sat.

In the dark room, she rubbed oil on her hands and then started to rub my forehead for the next five minutes. With her thumb, she did the same motion over and over. I didn't have the slightest idea what she was doing. By the time she finished rubbing my forehead with her thumbs, I was ready to get out of the chair and get outside.

When I got outside, the mother smiled and went inside. Till this day, I can only assume the shaman did the same thing to the mother as well. When the mom came out about five minutes later, we made our trek back through the mud and back onto the main road.

When we got back to the house mid-afternoon the majority of the guests had already left. The mother and sister immediately started cleaning up the house and washing dishes. While the mother and sister were cleaning, I thought it would be really cool to teach the siblings and some of the cousins a poker game—five-card draw.

They grasped the concept after only a few minutes. There were times throughout the game I was feeling hustled.

I could not believe some of the hands they had and how easily they took my money. I started out the game with fifteen dollars on the table and had to buy in with another ten. Even though I lost my week's allowance in less than an hour, I still had fun sitting around the table with them playing cards.

I learned that day that the younger sister may appear all sweet and innocent at first glance, but once you have money at stake, she's a warrior. After a few hours of poker I was glad to hear the mother call for dinner.

Taking our seats around the eight-person table, I told the mother I wasn't going to be needing dinner tonight and I should save room for my dinner with Mazhenjie and my other orphanage buddies. Earlier that day I promised the guys I would go out to eat with them, as it would be my last night with them for a while.

With a half-angry look and a half-disappointed shrug she said, "Eat a little before you go." So before leaving their home, I made sure to try at least one bite of all the dishes and drink some soup. With a full belly already, I caught my ride into town and met with Mazhenjie at a hotpot restaurant where two other orphanage buddies and a girlfriend were waiting. When we took our seats and ordered plates of meat, lettuce, mushrooms, carrots and a bottle of beer, I dipped squid and mushrooms into a hot soy sauce, which felt like an explosion of fire in my mouth, putting me in enormous pain for the next ten minutes. Drinking cup after cup of water didn't quell the burning, so I grabbed the beer bottle and took a few drinks. That made it worse. With the guys laughing hysterically, I started to feel very lightheaded and a bit woozy, so I went to the bathroom to wash away the sweat on my face and cool off. When I returned from the bathroom, I was feeling a lot better and my mouth wasn't as hot as before.

There wasn't too much left for us to do that night. We had eaten our fill and laughed till we cried. It was a great way to end the night with great company. From the restaurant, I took a taxi back to my hotel and called it an early night.

My first night with the biological family. I am showing them the photos I took while searching for them.

CHAPTER 34

The night before my departure

On my last full day at Ma'anshan, I didn't want to do anything but hang out with the siblings and family for the majority of the day. I didn't care what we did or what we saw, it was just going to be a fun, relaxing day. I checked out of my hotel that morning and made my way toward Dangtu. It was a sunny beautiful morning. I was wearing a short sleeve shirt and jeans. The weather was perfect. When I got to the house, the mother was standing outside, cracking eggs and boiling soup. By this time, everybody in the village knew chicken soup was my favorite. I already had breakfast at the hotel, but the mom insisted I eat even more. It would have been futile to argue. She placed a large bowl of soup outside on the porch table with a little beer.

The mom said she was going into the village, so the brother and I followed. We walked along the patty fields and passed the neighbor's chicken coop onto the main road. From there we walked about ten minutes to the city village market. When I say "village market," I mean there were five stores, with maybe a few vegetable carts outside their building.

The mother went into the clothing store and I took the opportunity to meet and greet a few shop owners. When I was walking around, I passed by a building that was producing a lot of noise. Inside was a room filled with women sitting at sewing machines. I don't want to say it was a sweatshop, but it was a small room with a bunch of textiles lying all over the floor.

Smiling as I was looking inward, I just popped my head back out and walked away. I'm sure I had all those girls just giggling away. After looking around for a few more minutes, the mother came out from the store across the street holding a big winter jacket. Avoiding the chickens that were walking aimlessly along the road, I met up with the mom. She held up the jacket to my chest and sized me up. With a nod of approval, she unzipped the jacket and told me to put it on.

I did, and it fit perfectly. It was a very sweet gift. All throughout this trip meeting the family, I had gotten a lot of food and clothing. It almost seemed like they were trying to make up for the lost years. When we got back to the house, I saw my clothes wet and hanging on the wire above the porch. My Nike shoes no longer had mud on them and were drying in the sun. I even saw my rock-and-roll boxer briefs hanging out for everyone to see. How embarrassing! I'm glad I didn't have anything too personal in my bag.

As my clothes were drying, some uncles and cousins came over to play poker. The family noticed that I had a really nice camera and asked that we got a good picture before it was too dark, so we all gathered for a family portrait.

Even though I was staying at the family's house my last night, I still had one more person I had to see before returning to Taiwan—Lisa.

At seven I was outside her door. Before I rang the doorbell, I did a quick pit sniff and then pushed the button. When she answered, I opened the screen door and took my shoes off before entering. As I was doing that, I could see, to my right, two glasses of red wine and biscuits on a platter.

We took our seats and toasted to the successful end of my quest. It was such a nice conversation filled with laughter, secrets and some tears. I babbled on and on about my family in the U.S. and my biological family.

We talked about fate and how none of this would have happened had it not been for the guard at the radio station calling the police. After a few glasses of wine and more laughs, I looked at my watch and realized I needed to get myself into a cab before it got too late to find one. I was a sad boy at that moment because I had to say goodbye to the one person who made this all happen.

I followed her to the kitchen with both glasses in hand and said, "Thank you for such a nice evening." When I walked to the door, I proceeded to grab my shoes; then I did the first thing my heart wanted to do all night. I turned around and kissed her. With a smile on her face and my heart pounding faster and faster, I found myself at a loss for words. With her lips still fresh on mine, I didn't know what else to do but grab my stuff and leave.

Getting into that taxi was a challenge in itself. I knew the only thing separating her from me was a door. I climbed into a taxi, but wanted to jump out and run back to Lisa. But I held steady, starring at her apartment window and whispering goodbye. I arrived back to Dangtu about midnight with the brother, his fiancé and the sister still up chewing seeds and playing cards. I pulled up a seat and joined in with their conversation. It was about this time that the father and mother both exited their rooms to check up on us. The first thing the mother asked was, "Did you eat?" Explaining to her exactly what I ate and with whom, she nodded her head in disapproval and exited. After ten minutes or so, she returned with a big bowl of chicken soup. Even though I was full, I was going to enjoy the tender delicious chicken leg soaked in broth for as long as I could. A big smile with chicken in my teeth was the only thing the mother needed to feel better.

As I took my last sip of soup, the mother came back into the house with a nine-foot sugar cane and a butcher's knife. She cut and peeled the cane into one-foot sections and handed them out for us to enjoy. Wondering what I was supposed to do with it or how I was supposed to eat it, I watched the brother as he dug his teeth into the sugar cane. I was half amazed and half scared how fast he was eating the sugar cane. He was like a beaver.

I took a small bite of my sugar cane and gave it a good suck. It was an explosion of sweetness. As I took a bite into it, the first layer was a little stiff, but the inside was really soft and chewy. It was absolutely wonderful and surprising, much like these people and this land. It looked rough on the outside, but the inside was sweet. With some chewing and sucking of the juices, the brother took a break from his and said, "Don't swallow the outside." I asked what I was supposed to do with the scraps in my mouth. He said, "Just spit it on the ground and Mom will clean it later." When I had a chance to compose myself, I told him if I were to do that in the U.S., my mom would take the sugar cane and hit me over the head with it.

With my hand really sticky from the sugar cane and my teeth really sore from gnawing, I was done. With clean hands all around and full bellies, the family and I took a seat around the table. We had such natural conversation. I told them what some of my favorite memories were from childhood. I told them stories of how my sister and I caused so much mischief. I even told them stories about my old girlfriends and what went wrong.

I felt relaxed, as if conversing with old friends. We talked about the father's job and the mother's responsibilities with the rice field. We talked about the brother's massage job and how he met his fiancée there. I learned that the sister was a waitress at a restaurant and had been there for quite some time. The father worked for a company in a province called Hangzhou. From the sound of it, he cleaned shoes on a factory line. The father was also telling me how he rarely got to come home—usually for a few days during the Chinese New Year. The company he worked for provided living accommodations for the workers so they could save more money.

The mother worked at home tending to the family rice fields. She grew rice to feed the family, so she had a very big incentive to make sure the rice fields have high yields. I could tell she worked very hard year round. What worried me most was how hard they work for very little in return. I wished they could relax and take a break. But the truth is they worked to survive. After telling me what work life was like in China, they asked me what the working conditions were like in the U.S. I explained the concept of minimum wage. I think they were pretty blown away that Oregon's minimum wage was eight dollars and fifty cents an hour. The brother then asked how much I earned working at my last summer job. Let's just say, I made in three months more than what the brother makes a year. I told him that a normal college student makes about that twenty-five hundred dollars a summer.

The mother went into her room and emerged with two coins. "In our family there are four of these coins; your sister and brother both have one, and now you will have one. Once you get married you will receive the fourth and last coin that my mother passed down to me. The brother jumped into the mix and said, "These coins are not to be traded or sold, this coin needs to stay in your family and be passed down for generations to come."

I was feeling overwhelmed with happiness. I was now part of this family's—my birth family's—lineage. Between sniffs and composing myself, I said thank you and that it meant a lot to me to receive such a precious gift. Holding the coin in my hand, I examined its every grove and rubbed each rivet with my finger. The more I looked at, the more I cried. I also expressed how happy and blessed my family and I in the U.S. are because of what my birth family did. The abandonment resulted in a wonderful life for me in the U.S., and parents so supportive and kind that they financed my quest to discover my true past. I was blessed with a second chance at having a great life. "Thank you for giving me a life that I can be proud of," I told the family.

At this point, it was four in the morning and I was more ready for some shut-eye. In my bedroom was a nice bucket of toiletries for me to use and a couple of towels for me to wash my face with. With the mother's assistance, I brushed my teeth and applied my nightly acne cream. When I went back to my room, the brother had filled the bucket with lukewarm water and was patiently waiting for my return. He told me to sit and then started to roll up my jean pants.

Little tickles and twitches in the leg later, the brother washed my feet and legs. I was sitting on the bed thinking to myself, This is the weirdest bedtime ritual I have had. The brother is cleaning my feet and the father is in my bed warming it up for me. Don't judge it, just let it happen. Seconds after rolling my pant legs down, the brother started to clean my face with the very rag he just cleaned my feet with. They were grooming me as if I were a pampered pet.

I can see we both inherited big smiles.

CHAPTER 35

Oh, boy!!

The siblings and I learned throughout our time together that we all have a common interest in the sport of badminton. What better way to end the trip than to play a friendly match? The brother wasn't that skilled, but the sister could play. In fact, the sister challenged me to a duel for the title. It was now a battle between China and the U.S.A.

I drew a line in the dirt and told her this was the net and not to cross it. The rules were set and she started by serving. I could tell just after a few minutes this was going to be a close game. I do think however, with the combination of my grunting and other obnoxious distractions, I had the upper hand.

With the score tied and sweat dripping from both our faces,

we were both feeling the intensity. Her match point serve was high with a lot of speed. As I looked up preparing to hit the birdie with all my strength, the sun caused me to squint. Not only did I miss the birdie entirely but I also managed to fall down the rock hill causing some scrapes and cuts on my forearm.

The sister and brother quickly ran over to help me up and dust me off when I just started laughing. I couldn't help but laugh too and ask the sister for a rematch. Once I got dusted off and wiped away the blood, I took a breather and found a seat on the porch looking out into the field. I could see rice fields, grapevines, big houses, old houses, and tall beautiful mountains. It was such a peaceful atmosphere. I could see myself in 70 years in a rocking chair and bathrobe, watching the days go by. The three of us took a break from badminton and ate some sugar cane on the porch. I saw the father in the distance walking away from the house. I put the sugar cane down and ran after him. We made small talk about fishing and the sports I played while growing up. I enjoyed telling him about my family's annual camping trip and the fishing trips my father and I frequently took when I was a kid.

The father enjoyed hearing more about my future, how I was going to reach my dreams. I told him, "The only thing that matters right now is for me to make enough money to build two houses."

The two houses would share the same backyard, with a pool for me to enjoy my adult beverages. My mom and dad would live in one of the houses and I in the other. I was dead serious when I told him, but he laughed anyway.

So, here we were, walking side by side, the two of us jumping from one patty field to another trying to find the main road. Once we got to the main road, we arrived at a few produce stands. While the father picked out the chickens he wanted to buy, I walked as far away as I could to avoid seeing them butchered.

In my backpack were some Taiwanese and U.S. coins. I

handed out most of the coins as gifts to the merchants, who were grateful and excited to get U.S. currency. When we got back to the house, I handed the mother her freshly killed and plucked chicken and rejoined the siblings. I couldn't visit with them too long considering I still needed to re-pack my bag before leaving for the airport. When I went into my room to start organizing my belongings, I saw one of the aunts rolling up my underwear and folding my shirts. When I got closer to the room, the mother handed me a red envelope.

Knowing well enough what comes in red envelopes, I refused to accept the money. I could tell inside the envelope held about five hundred U.S. dollars. I was not going to accept such a generous gift from the family, especially because of how much they had already done for me. I put my arms up and refused in a polite manner, "No, no and no. I don't want your money; all I want is your friendship." Just when I thought I won the battle, reinforcements came in the room to assist the mother.

Not only did I have the mother cornering me and trying to force the money into my pocket, but also the father, brother, sister and even the old sweet Nana forcing the envelope in my pocket.

I didn't know what to do but accept defeat and say thank you. I placed the envelope in a safe place in my backpack and resumed packing. This was a hugely generous gift from such poor people. I felt guilty and flattered. I was wrong about the amount. There was nearly eight hundred dollars in that envelope. Just imagine: a family that nineteen years earlier abandoned a child because of financial strains was now handing over six to nine months' worth of their annual earnings. I was blown away. This money could have bought them more than one hundred and twenty adult chickens; eight hundred bottles of hard liquor, with enough left for both kids' wedding portraits. Instead they gave it to me to help pay for my education. The ironic part of all this is, in the beginning, I was afraid that they were going to ask me for money.

As I was just about to close up my bag, I heard the sister's boyfriend talk about the travel time needed to get to the airport. I needed to be at the airport in two and a half hours and the drive there would take two. Rushing out the door with my backpack, I told the family, "We have to leave now or I am going to miss my flight."

When the family realized the time crunch we were in, we sorted who was going to ride in what vehicle with whom. We took two cars. I waved goodbye to the extended family and yelled, "Thank you!" as we pulled away.

About every ten minutes I asked the boyfriend, "Are we close? How far now? Do you think we will make it in time?" I was having a panic attack worrying that I would miss my flight. I was starting to think they were intentionally making me late. I knew that wasn't true, but we kept getting separated. At one point the car behind us missed a turn and was heading in the wrong direction. After waiting for five minutes, I said, "We need to go now. They will just have to meet us there. I can at least get checked in." Getting back on the freeway was good and I felt I could still make it with minutes to spare. Not too long after taking the off-ramp, I could see jets landing and taking off.

Just as we started to see the terminal and were about to pull into the parking lot, the boyfriend pulled over just outside entrance gate to wait for the second vehicle to catch up. I quickly got out of the car and said, "Okay, wait for the other car and I will run to check in."

I ran as fast as I could, avoiding cars and trolleys, in hopes of reaching the ticket counter. Just as I was about to enter the International Departure Gate, I heard a voice yelling my name. I instantly stopped and looked around and saw Lisa and a couple of reporters on the second level.

I pointed to my door and ran through it looking for the Dragon Air kiosk. Running from one end to the other, I couldn't find the right kiosk. Caught up in the moment, I forgot I needed to go through a security checkpoint. I sprinted through it and found my counter. Just as I thought I made it, I realized my passport was in my bag, which was still in the car. The lady at the counter said I had about five minutes before the flight check-in service was closed.

So, I ran out of the security point and ran into Lisa. Not having time to explain, I asked where the brother was with my bag. The four of us were on our phones calling the family. I was finally able to connect with the brother and attempted to explain my current location. But even with the detailed explanation of my location, he was lost.

At one point, one of the reporters started to yell his name real loud in the airport hoping he would hear his voice. Not much later, after a break from yelling, I spotted my yellow backpack outside on the brother's shoulders. I jumped the bench and ran through the sliding doors to grab the passport. I snatched the booklet and ran with Lisa back through the security gate to find the check-in counter. It was too late. All of the running and the screaming was not enough. I missed the check-in time by ten minutes and wasn't allowed to board the plane.

I wasn't angry with the family or the drivers, but I was frustrated at myself for not checking the time needed beforehand. Still standing in front of the service counter, I was introduced to the manager on duty to help resolve my flight schedule. In a short time, I was printed a new ticket. I would now be flying out the following morning.

CHAPTER 36

Real men cry

I knew that I couldn't stay in Dangtu for the night, and I needed to start my readings for the class I had the following day. So, I told the family that the flight had been changed and that I needed to get a hotel. They were very understanding about my situation and were happy to leave me be for the duration of the day.

I insisted that I take a taxi back to Ma'anshan and we say our goodbyes now so they didn't have to return tomorrow morning at the crack of dawn. They wanted to hear none of it; in fact, they insisted on staying in a friend's home for the evening in Ma'anshan so they could take me to the airport the following morning. Hesitant to accept their offer, I yielded.

Ignoring my better judgment, I said, "Okay," and planned what tomorrow would look like. When all was said, done and planned, the parents, sister and I got in a car and headed toward Ma'anshan. The boyfriend was driving and the father was sitting in the passenger's seat. I was situated between the mother and the sister. When we left the airport parking lot, I asked the sister if she wanted to talk to my mother in the States.

I, of course, paid no attention to the clock or time difference, so when I called Hermiston, Oregon, it was around eleven at night there. As I pulled out my Blackberry, I dialed my mom's cell phone number and then put the phone on speaker. After a few rings, my mom picked up in a frantic voice and asked if I was okay. I said that I was fine and enjoying my time here.

I asked why she sounded so panicked. It turns out I made a few mistakes while in China: I failed to call mom when I arrived in China; I failed to give my mom my Chinese cell phone number; I hadn't checked in with friends and roommates at school. I had essentially been M.I.A. three days and people were worried. I explained that I didn't have access to a computer for three days and that using the cell phone would have been very expensive.

My dad had tried several different methods of trying to get ahold of me, but it was useless. To make things even worse, I stayed a day longer than what I originally told them. So, when they didn't hear from me the day I was supposed to arrive back in Taiwan, their fears exacerbated.

Needless to say, my mom was relieved to hear my voice and to know that I was okay. After receiving Mother's forgiveness, I put the phone back on speakerphone and allowed the sister to talk with my mom for a few minutes. The phone chat was brief due to the language barrier, but it was a lot of fun to hear the sister speak to my mom.

I did my best to translate what the sister wanted to say. The only problem was, she was so excited to speak to my mom, she spoke really fast and I wasn't able to catch everything. After a few minutes of talking and translating, I turned the speakerphone off and had a conversation with my mom.

It felt so good to be able to speak with Mother. I had so much to tell and I didn't know where to begin. I started by telling her how much the siblings and I look alike, followed by what my first day was like. I went on and on about the things I've been doing with the family and what I had planned next. I tried to go into great detail about the family's background and their occupations when I realized my mom was still half asleep and it was late in Oregon.

Not giving it much thought or consideration, I kept talking and talking, keeping my mom from sleeping. I know my mom would have stayed up all night just to hear my voice and to know I was safe. When my mom started to ask me questions about the family and their reasons for abandoning me I took a few deep breaths before explaining. As I was finishing answering her questions, I remember thinking to myself how difficult it was for them to leave me on that day in March of 1991. It no longer felt like abandonment. Rather, the mother and father wanted a better life for me than they could provide. It was a selfless act, not a selfish one.

Having said that, I wanted to make sure my mom understood I was doing okay and that she could start breathing again. I started off by telling her not to worry and that they were a really nice family. I know my mom was being the protective mother she has always been and was just making sure I was feeling comfortable and safe. It was about this time that I had a major breakdown and started to cry. I was in the middle of explaining what the family's intentions were. In a split second, I went from dry eyes to baby eyes. I broke down and lost a hold of my manhood. I had many tearful moments on the trip, but this was the first time I had cried with such intensity. The whole trip I had to be strong for myself and for those around me in order for me to stay in control. I had finally cracked. I don't know, maybe it was hearing my mom's voice for the first time in a week, but I let everything out. My cell phone bill was about one hundred and twenty dollars that month and eighty of that was me mumbling and crying on the phone to Mother. When I thought I was getting myself put back together, I started to cry again, except the sister and mother broke out in tears as well.

We pulled over at a little stand and bought a couple of ice

teas to cool me off. When we got back on the road, I told my mom about how the family felt about me and what they wanted from me. I couldn't find the words to describe at the time how the family felt about this new arrangement, but I did my best to explain myself during sniffles.

I told my mom, the parents' intentions were genuine and all they wanted was to see me as the person I am today. The father said, "If you have time, please come see us and let us know how you're doing, but if you don't have time, then be with your parents and stay in school. Work hard and study hard." I couldn't stop crying when I told her what the father had said and how he said it. It meant the world. The last thing I said to the sister when they dropped me at the hotel was that "Real men do cry." At last, we pulled up to the hotel and I proceeded to get out.

CHAPTER 37

Cheers!

Now that my studies were finally caught up, the only thing left for me to do was get some shuteye. I had no problem getting to sleep that night. The second my head hit the pillow, I was dead to the world. While I was dreaming about being chased by a group of hooligans, I was pulled from my unconscious state to full alertness when my cell phone went off.

Looking at the clock, then back at my cell phone, I was wondering who was calling me at such an early hour. I pulled the sheets away and then grabbed my cell phone off the dresser. I stared at the screen trying to figure out whose number this was. The voice that soon followed was quiet and hesitant.

I asked if he could speak a little louder. He repeated what he just said and it didn't take me another second to recognize the voice. I asked the father if everything was okay and why he was calling so freaking early.

The second I heard everything was okay, I interrupted him and said, "I'm sorry, but it is four in the morning and I have to wake up in two hours. I will talk to you soon. Good night." When

I got off the phone with the father, I couldn't stop wondering why he would call me so early. Was everything really okay or was there a bigger issue at hand? I tried not to think too much about the call, but it still lingered in my head for a while. When my brain started to slow down, I was finally able to fall back asleep.

After what seemed to be just ten more minutes of sleep, the hour hand was on six already and I had to start getting ready. I took a shower, brushed my teeth, did a pimple check and then changed into my clothes. I was running a little late, so I started to pick up the pace. The family had patiently been waiting for me in the lobby. We got in the car and left for Nanjing Airport. The car was packed. The father was sitting in the passenger's seat, the sister was sitting on the mother's lap and the girlfriend was sitting on the brother's lap on the right of me. Needless to say, we had a very cozy ride to the airport. When we got situated so we were somewhat comfortable, the sister handed me a box wrapped in pink tissue.

Touched that she gave me a gift, I opened the gift and pulled out a ceramic frog mug. It was a very cute mug that had frog designs on the side and even included a frog spoon that matched the cup. I gave her a hug and said, "Whenever I use this, I will always think of you."

In the car, the family asked if I knew when I would be able to return. I was honest. "The future is unclear for me right now, but when I get a chance, I will be sure to return." That answer seemed to be good enough for them; all they cared about was that I wanted to return. I leaned forward in my seat and patted the father on the shoulder to ask if we could have a private conversation once we arrived at the airport.

I was reluctant to ask why the father called me so early that morning. I had checked in and we still had plenty of time, so I looked at the father and asked if now was a good time to have a private conversation.

So, the father in his dark blue overcoat and I with my

backpack walked for a few minutes discussing various topics. While some of the time involved me talking or him talking, there were also moments of silence. As we were walking, I could see the mother closely following behind us cracking boiled eggs for me to eat. It was quite humorous when I ate the first egg and saw she still had about nine more in a bag. I told her one egg is enough and that my belly was full. Still insisting that I eat more eggs, she gave me another, and then cracked a third. Finally the father looked at her and said, "No more. Let us be."

The father instructed me to give the letter to my parents in the U.S. to thank them for raising me. When I promised to safely guard the letter and to give my family the letter the moment I saw them, he nodded his headed and didn't say another word.

After tucking away the letter, I asked the father why he called the night before so early. He said he was worried about the emotional breakdown I had the previous day in the car. I smiled and said, "I'm fine now. I just needed to talk with my mom."

He said he couldn't sleep and had a lot on his mind. I asked if he wanted to talk about it and if there was anything I could help him with. As the strong brave man he is, he said no. As we were about to rejoin the group, he pulled my shirt and instructed me to wait for a moment.

Turning around and watching the father's eyes tear up, I handed him a tissue and reassured him everything was all right. Still not knowing what was on his mind or what he wanted to say, I gave him a moment to compose himself and waited to give him another opportunity to speak. He looked at me and said, "I'm sorry."

I knew what he was sorry about, but I didn't know what to say. How could I be angry at the parents for abandoning me, especially after I think about the life I have now in the U.S.? All I could say at the time was, "Don't be sorry, be grateful." I put my hand on his shoulder and told him, "Because of what you guys did, I now have an education. Because of what you guys did nineteen years ago, I now have a bright future that I can call my own. Because of what you guys did, I have a family that loves me, supports me and pushes me to be a stronger and a better person every day."

I added, "Don't be sorry. Be happy for being able to help provide a second chance for me. I should be saying thank you, and I know my family in the U.S. is grateful every day for the gift you gave them." I was trying not to have a repeat of the day before, but I couldn't help but have tears of happiness and joy fall from my eyes and onto my shoes.

He looked at me one more time and said, "You tell your family every day you love them and you use this second chance that you've been given and you make the best of it." He continued to say, "Go to school, study hard and make a life for yourself." If I had learned anything about the father, it is that he is very stoic but kind. He is a strong man with a soft heart, a person who shows compassion but not weakness. As I was still trying to pull myself together in front of the family, the mother chased after the father to console him. Losing track of time, all I heard was my flight announced over the intercom. I quickly grabbed my bag and said to the family, "Let's not make it another nineteen years."

I gave the family hugs and said thank you once more for everything they did. When the hugs were given and tears were falling, I walked toward security. Waving goodbye as I got closer and closer to the metal detector, I turned around and handed my ticket to the security guard. He gave me a confused look and pointed to a different line.

With everything happening at the time, I didn't even realize I was in the domestic line. I quickly asked where the international line was, and was pointed back to the international check-in kiosk area. Thinking to myself, I don't remember seeing this sort of thing by the check-in area, but not in a position to question anybody and with my backpack digging into my shoulders. I sprinted back out of the line and flew right past the family once more. I said, "Wrong line!" as I dashed by.

Looking at my watch, I still had thirty minutes before takeoff. I handed the passport and plane ticket to the officer and looked back one more time to wave goodbye to my brother. As I was standing in line with just a steel bar separating my brother from me, I smiled and gave him one more wave goodbye.

The last moments with him in my sight just seemed to be all in slow motion. It was almost like every movement we made lasted forever. His wave goodbye and his smile to me seemed to have made a lasting impression. It was almost like a flashback of the past eighteen days of searching had finally led to this point in time. I had a sense of knowing and closure.

A Taiwanese TV program that helped get my story out there and raise funds for the foundation.

CHAPTER 38

My second chance

I was lucky in China, very lucky. This adventure, this trip, this dream I had lived has meant so much to my family in the U.S., my family in China and, of course, to me. My entire life I always wondered what life in China was like and if I would ever return. A part of me always wondered if I had my father's nose or my mother's eyes.

Throughout my teenage years growing up in the States, I was asked on a regular basis if I ever wanted to meet my biological parents. Maybe it was my age or my lack of understanding of the world, but I said, "No. I have no desire in my heart to meet the people who abandoned me." I was living the life that every child strives for: great set of parents, family vacations producing joyful memories, wonderful group of friends and TV cartoons for me to watch after homework was done.

However, as I started to grow up, my thirst for knowledge about my biological parents intensified. I was beginning to think and feel it was the right time in my life to start this search. I had so little to start from. I knew only basic information about the orphanage and the name of the town where I was found. I knew this search was going to be nearly impossible. The only thing I could count on was my parents' support from the very beginning to the very end. So with my parents' love and support I was ready to try.

On just the first day alone, my trip surpassed all expectations. I had the opportunity I always wanted, and that was to walk the streets of Ma'anshan. I got to see not only the orphanage I was in, but I also had the privilege of re-uniting with my orphan siblings. That alone was a successful search. Having the ability to hear stories of my youth and memories we shared together were priceless moments.

After meeting them, I knew I had already found a family in Ma'anshan. Not only did I get the chance to meet my orphan buddies, but I also had the opportunity to learn about the great things Ma'anshan Welfare Institute does on a daily basis. I don't think I can say it enough; I am so blessed and touched by everyone's generosity throughout my time there. It has been just a wonderful, rewarding experience and I can't thank everybody enough for everything they did. That includes the wonderful and generous people of Ma'anshan who embraced me and heralded my cause.

I often speak of this story as a butterfly effect. I was in the right place at the right time. Had I not met He Li Juan at the airport, I wouldn't have been at a coffee shop by the radio station. Had I not gone when I did, I might not have had the same run-in as I did with the security guard. Of course, if I hadn't had that confrontation with the guard, then I wouldn't have met Lisa, and the rest is history. I know without a doubt if it wasn't for FM 92.8 or Massi Newspaper Company, this search could have had a different outcome.

Call it fate or whatever you want, but it was written in my life that I would meet Lisa that night. Meeting Lisa didn't just mean finding my biological family; it meant inspiring thousands in Ma'anshan.

Meeting my birth family and seeing where they lived was a dream I never thought was possible. After returning to my normal life in the U.S. and taking the time to absorb everything, I don't think I could be more thankful for how lucky I am with this family. All my worries about my biological family are no longer an issue.

Before I traveled to Ma'anshan to meet the family, my grandfather Richard Harris called me one evening to talk about my upcoming trip. He said, "Grandma Priscilla and I talked about it for a while and would like you to give them a gift in our name." The gift was to be made at my discretion and only if I wanted to give it. My grandparents wanted to show their appreciation toward the family for keeping me alive and taking care of me for as long as they did. "Thank you both for your offer, Grandpa, but all I know is I don't want to give them a gift or any money." I continued to explain how I felt toward the family and that I strongly felt they didn't deserve a gift.

I was also afraid if I gave them a gift or money, they would just want more. I was trying to protect my family, my family's money, and myself. When all was said and done, I said to Grandpa, "This family doesn't deserve a single thing from me." Now with the wisdom of hindsight, I see how much of a jerk I sounded like back then. As the trip progressed and I spent more time with the birth family, my feelings morphed from they deserve nothing into they deserve everything.

I can't even start to describe how much happiness the birth family brought to my life in that week we spent together. The family knows about me now, and now I know about them. I heard the answers I needed to hear to find closure in regard to my first four years and now I can move forward.

The greatest part of reuniting with my biological family that I will take away is learning how genuine and honest they all were. Each individual family member, the birth parents, the biological siblings, aunts, uncles, and other blood relatives, spoke from their hearts and poured out their true feelings. There was never a point in the trip where I felt manipulated or taken advantage of. Except in the poker games, which I taught them to play.

They made sure I was comfortable and offered me nothing but kindness. Even with everything said, the family didn't make me feel guilty about returning to the U.S. In fact, that's what made this trip so comfortable. Never was there a moment when I ever forgot who my real parents were and who took me in as one of their own. I knew that and my adoptive parents know that. The biological parents knew they weren't my emotional parents and they understood that both my life and my family are in the United States.

My parents taught me the lack of importance of titles and to accept a different definition of family. Blood does not determine the mother or father to a child, nor does having the same DNA strand make a stronger bond of a mother's love for her son. But this trip taught me that whether a sister and brother come from two different parts of the world or not, they will still fight and love as normal brothers and sisters do.

It's amazing how a simple idea or photo that I looked at five years earlier led me to this point right now. It goes to show that nothing is impossible or out of reach. I took a challenge that my family and I both thought might be impossible and yet managed to succeed. How did I succeed? I had hope. Hope and following my heart has led me to where I am today. My mother and father have always said, "Listen to your heart on and off the court." That's exactly what I did then and what I will always do.

I have learned that with a heart filled with hope and a little luck, anything is possible and the lost can be found.

For all those kids out there who were adopted, whether from another country or from another family down the street, I can only say one thing: Find your own way of showing your family just how much they mean to you. Because no matter what happens, those people who took you in or watched your soccer game in the freezing cold will always be there for you. From the bottom of my heart, I beg that you never forget the gift that your family gave you.

For you parents who adopted, I just want to say thank you for changing a child's life. Thank you for seeing past the deformities we may have or the expenses you incur when adopting. Thank you for being there for us when we needed you the most.

With our new addition, Marie!

EPILOGUE

To this day, I still talk to my biological family regularly. The brother started his own little family with a baby boy in February of 2013.

He is now in a different city with his son and wife, working. They don't have Internet, but about once a month I get an update or phone call from the brother checking in or asking how I've been doing.

My biological sister is married now and will, I am certain, soon have a child of her own. Everything is still the same for my biological parents. The father is in Hangzhou working at a shoe factory, and the mom is working diligently on the family farm.

I took Mom's suggestion about writing a book. I built it around many of the emails I sent to my family and friends almost every night I was in China. Weeks after returning to Taiwan,

I was sitting in front of a publisher, handing them my emails. After an agreement, a contract was written up.

Three months after meeting them, the manuscript was finished and being translated into Chinese. China Times in Taiwan published my story and got the book circulating around the island by the end of that year. Soon after the book's release I started the most exciting project I could think of.

I was able to start The Second Chance Foundation, offering orphan kids opportunities to study abroad. It will also fund school supplies and shelter for Chinese children in orphanages. With the donation of all the royalties from book sales and various other donations, this foundation has raised hundreds of thousands of dollars. With this money and the assistance of Rotary International, we were able to offer Kobe, an orphan from Taiwan, an opportunity to study here in the United States in 2012. Kobe would be just the first exchange student we fund.

In the last two years, I have spoken at over a hundred Rotary meetings and various other organizations, trying to spread the word about the foundation. While at these events, I emphasize the need for more adoption and the need to give second chances. In June of 2012, I graduated from the University of Oregon with a degree in International Business and Chinese. As a graduate from Oregon, I was fortunate enough to be one of three commencement speakers talking about this story and the foundation. I also decided to release my book in the U.S. through Virginia-based publisher Koehler Books. As with the Chinese edition, sales from this book will be donated to the foundation. While I may not know what's next for me, I will do as I have always done and follow my heart with everything I do, both on and off the court.

Showing off with a poster of the Chinese version of my book.

Launching the book in Taiwan.

The site of the stadium where I was abandoned is now a park where I played.

Sharing a meal with old friends.

Hanging out with new friends.

Enjoying the festivities as a family.

The day my search turned into a citywide effort.

Enjoying sugar cane for the first time.

A happy reunion.

CPSIA information can be obtained at www.ICGtesting.com
Printed in the USA
BVOW08s0330261113

337365BV00006B/152/P